How to
Movie

with colored pencils

Copyright © 2017 by Jasmina Susak
www.jasminasusak.com

Jasmina Susak
Colored Pencil Artist
Author

How to draw realistic movie characters with colored pencils   Page 1

Table of contents:

Introduction.. 2
How to use this book …................................... 5
Tools... 6
Iron Man... 13
Deadpool... 61
About Artist …... 108

Introduction

This book will take you through the process of drawing two pictures of movie characters with colored pencils; Iron Man and Deadpool.
You'll learn how to work on shading with multiple nuances of a single colored pencil and these shading

techniques will give your pictures depth and a life-like appearance.

This book also covers techniques for creating textures like leather and shiny metal that are traditionally difficult to draw realistically in pencil. You'll learn tips for blending colors and creating subtle gradients, plus alternative approaches, like blending with a white pencil. It also explains the importance of sketching out areas you might need corrected with a graphite pencil first. And you will learn to use a simple oval shape to create proportional sketches without a reference photo.

While this book has an incredible amount of detail, including step-by-step drawings and explanations, sometimes words just aren't enough to explain a drawing. I have included links to time-lapse videos so you can compare your notes to the book while you watch me creating these drawings.

Drawing well is based on continued practice and patience and this book provides endless opportunities to develop your technique.

You don't have to rush through each tutorial - it's important to take time to get each step right before moving on. Beginners and advanced artists who want to further develop the subtleties of their technique will both benefit from the lessons and instructions on what and how to practice.

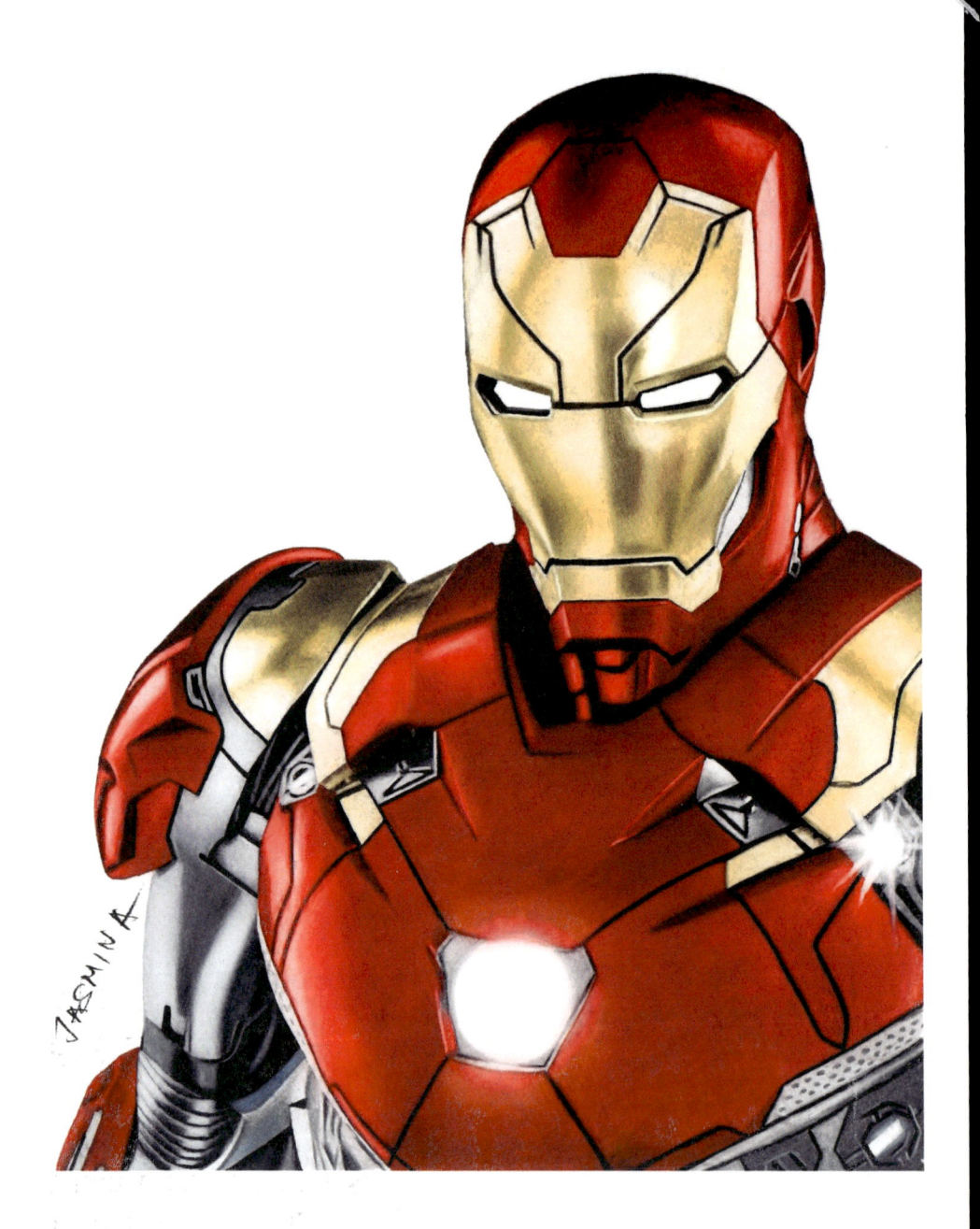

Iron Man Mark XLVII
Colored pencils, 8" x 11"

How to draw realistic movie characters with colored pencils

How to use this book

This book contains a picture and short explanation of each step for each drawing. I recommend you thoughtfully analyze the step, comparing the previous and next steps to see the exact differences between them. The more time you spend drawing, the better the result will be, so don't move to the next step until you are satisfied with the step you are currently working on. It's also best not to rush - if a drawing seems difficult, leave it for the next day. You don't have to finish a whole drawing in one go. I often spend two to three hours a day over five or six days on a single drawing.

If you draw on big sheets of with sharp pencils, it will be easier for you to produce more detailed pictures. I used A3 (30 cm x 40 cm/11.7" x 16.5") for these, but if you used A5 (5" x 8") or smaller, you just wouldn't have space for the details.

Patience and commitment are the most important skills of drawing. If you want success, you have to work on drawing with patience; loving and enjoying what you do, and doing it for yourself in the first place.

Having said that, if a drawing goes bad and you can't figure out what's wrong with it, throw it away and start a new one.

Lastly, the most important thing: *Practice*!

Tools

If you are still thinking about which medium to use to create your art, I want to convince you to choose colored pencils.

Colored pencils have many benefits. They allow precision, control of detail and depth. You can work lightly for a soft look or with many layers get the oil painting effect you see in most of my drawings. Additionally, they are very easy to carry, and you can work almost anywhere. It is an economical medium, and you don't need many extra supplies. Even if you buy the most expensive colored pencils (that I highly recommend) you will still spend less than to stock up with markers, oil paint, airbrush and other tools. Working with colored pencil requires little space, no drying time and creates no fumes or chemicals – except for the fixative that's used when your work is complete. Not to mention that when you gently touch the paper with colored pencil, nothing happens, which is not the case when working with markers, oil paint, or watercolors... You have full control, and this is what I like the most about colored pencils.

When talking about **sharpeners**, I don't recommend any brand or expensive sharpener. For me, the most important is to always have a new sharpener. Since I draw a lot, I sharpen a lot, so I use a single sharpener for about two weeks, and then I get a new one.

Colored pencils cannot be fully erased, so I use a **graphite pencil** for sketching and for making sure that the dark areas are in the right place before applying Black or another dark colored pencil.

However, you can improve or erase light colored pencils with an electric **eraser**. I often create highlights over the areas that I've drawn with dark colored pencils, using a battery operated eraser. This eraser is really helpful and the tips last a long time. It is really quiet, so you can use it in the presence of your pet (my three cats approve it :). I use a Helix eraser that is available at Amazon for only $10, including 10 eraser tips.

Colored pencils

If you want to draw colorful, realistic drawings like mine, you might also look for the tools I use.

I use **Prismacolor Premier** pencils. They are high quality professional-grade colored pencils that are not overly expensive, are smooth to work with and provide a lot of nuance. The pencils are really soft and can be easily spread over the paper.

The waxy buttery texture of the lead makes it ideal for

blending, burnishing and layering color to create the perfect mix. Prismacolor Premier provides palette of 150 colors, which is a really great deal. The more colors you have, the easier your job will be.

You can also buy an **individual single colored pencil**, which is a really good deal. You can also find the links on my website. This is also good, if you have used up only one pencil from your set, you can get that pencil without having to buy the full set again.

If you want to buy the complete set or **individual** Prismacolor Premier pencils, check out the product links to Amazon selling pages on my website:
http://jasminasusak.com/artsupplies/
Prismacolor pencils are so soft and behave so much unlike any other colored pencils on the market. When used correctly, Prismacolor drawings can take on the

appearance of a painting. They are perfect for blending and burnishing. Take a look at my drawings in the next image. These are drawn with Prismacolor Premier colored pencils only. Check out [my YouTube videos](#) to see how I drew all of these.

Many people complain that Prismacolor Premier pencils are easily broken. I don't have this experience at all. Here are two tips to avoid this. First, stop your pencil from breaking before you use it, for example, don't let them fall onto the floor. Even if the pencil doesn't break, the lead inside will. This can also happen

Deadpool
Colored pencils on grey paper, 8" x 11"

during manufacturing and shipping.

The second thing is to sharpen them gently. When sharpening, hold your pencil as close to the tip and sharpener as possible and sharpen slowly, not pushing it hard into the sharpener.

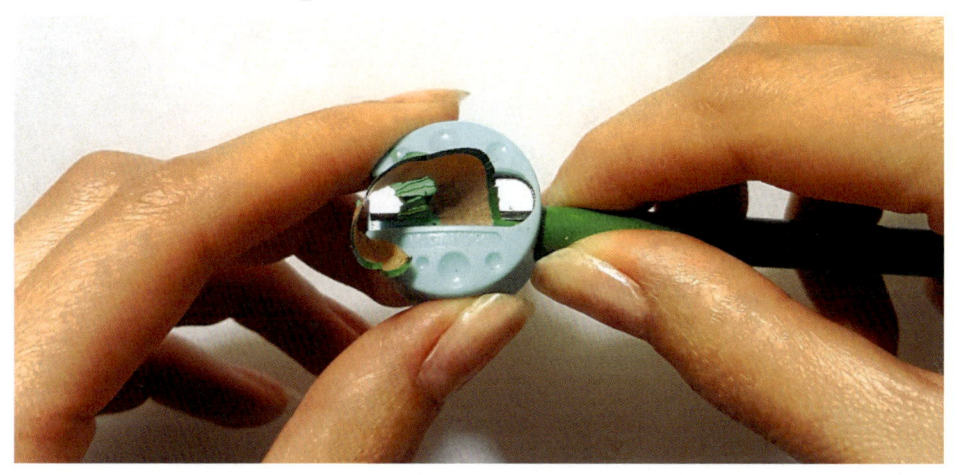

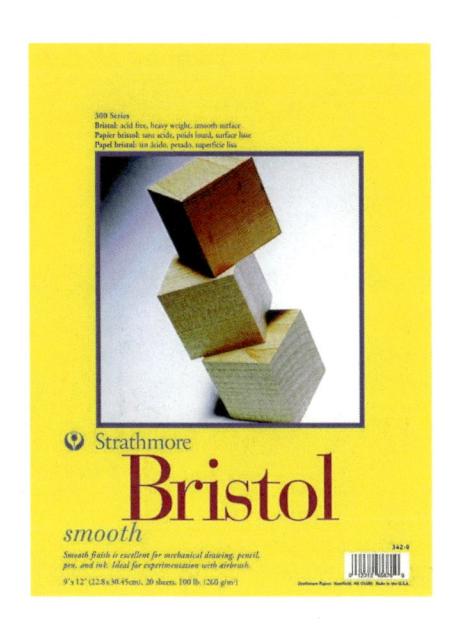

For these drawings you will need a good quality **paper**. Cheap sketch paper won't hold enough layers of pencil for a good finish. The right paper is very important, especially when you work in as many layers as I do. You can build up 20 layers, or even more, which is very hard on your paper and can cause the surface to tear or buckle. I recommend a smooth, fine toothed paper, such as Bristol. I suggest you choose bigger paper, so you can get much more detailed.

The **pencil lengthener** is a very useful tool that allows you to use almost every bit of a pencil before having to throw it away - very important when you are using pretty expensive pencils! It brings a feeling of balance and allows for a good grip. It securely holds round, triangular, and hexagonal pencils in its nickel-plated ferrule with a sliding ring.

The last half an inch or one centimeter of pencil will fall out of the lengthener, but you can superglue it to the end of a new pencil. Spread the glue on the ends that are to be glued and stick them together. Once it dries, or even better the next day, use and sharpen it just like a whole pencil. I usually glue it to a pencil that I rarely or never use. You can see in the next image how I resolve this.

Additionally, I use a white **ink gel pen** for small, shiny details, and **HB graphite pencil** for sketching.

Iron Man

First, draw an oval in the upper area of the piece of paper. If you want to draw just the head, draw your oval in the middle of the paper. The oval should be slightly narrower in the area of his chin, take a look at my oval in the next image and create the same.

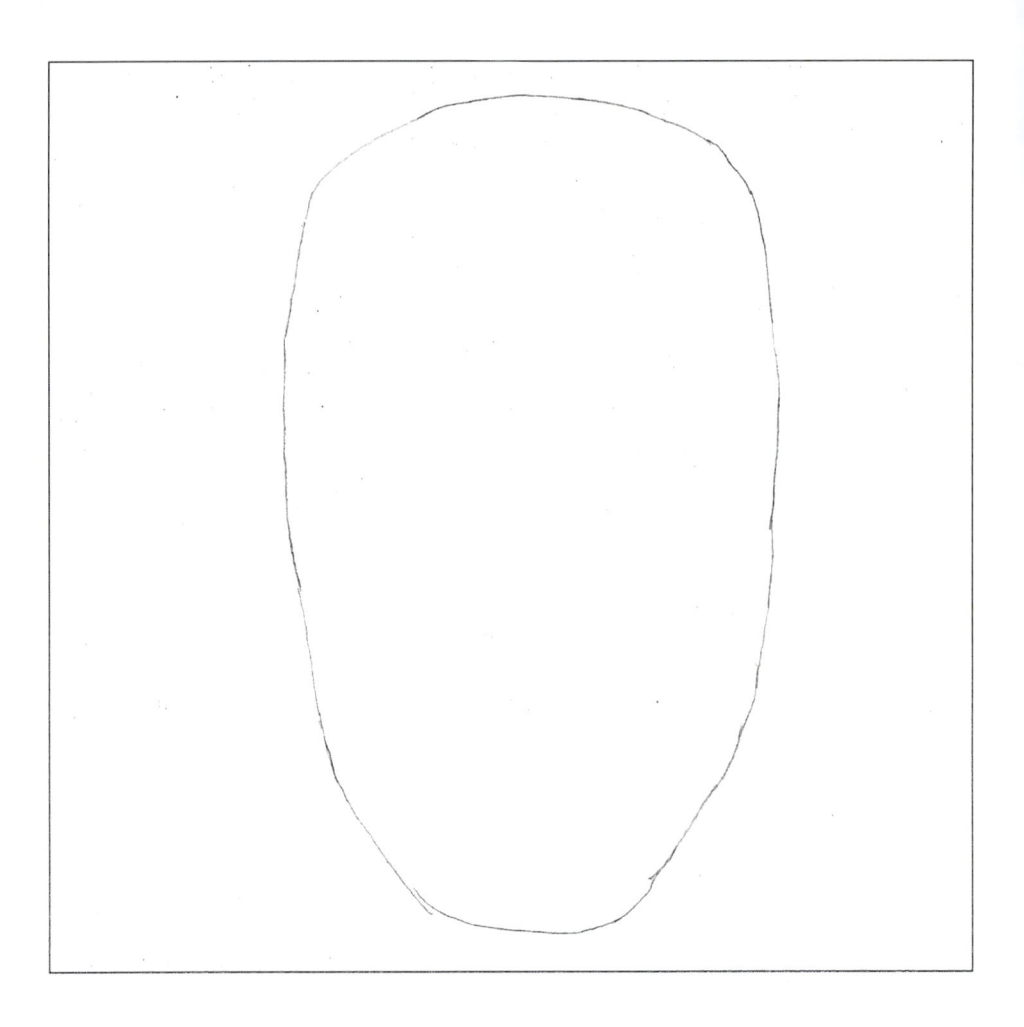

The next step is to divide the oval horizontally and vertically to guide the position of the eyes and the joins of the face mask sheeting.

Draw a vertical line to divide the oval in half, then a horizontal line (C) to divide the oval into quarters.

Draw two horizontal lines (A) and (B) above (C) to divide the upper half into thirds. Then another two (D) and (F) below.

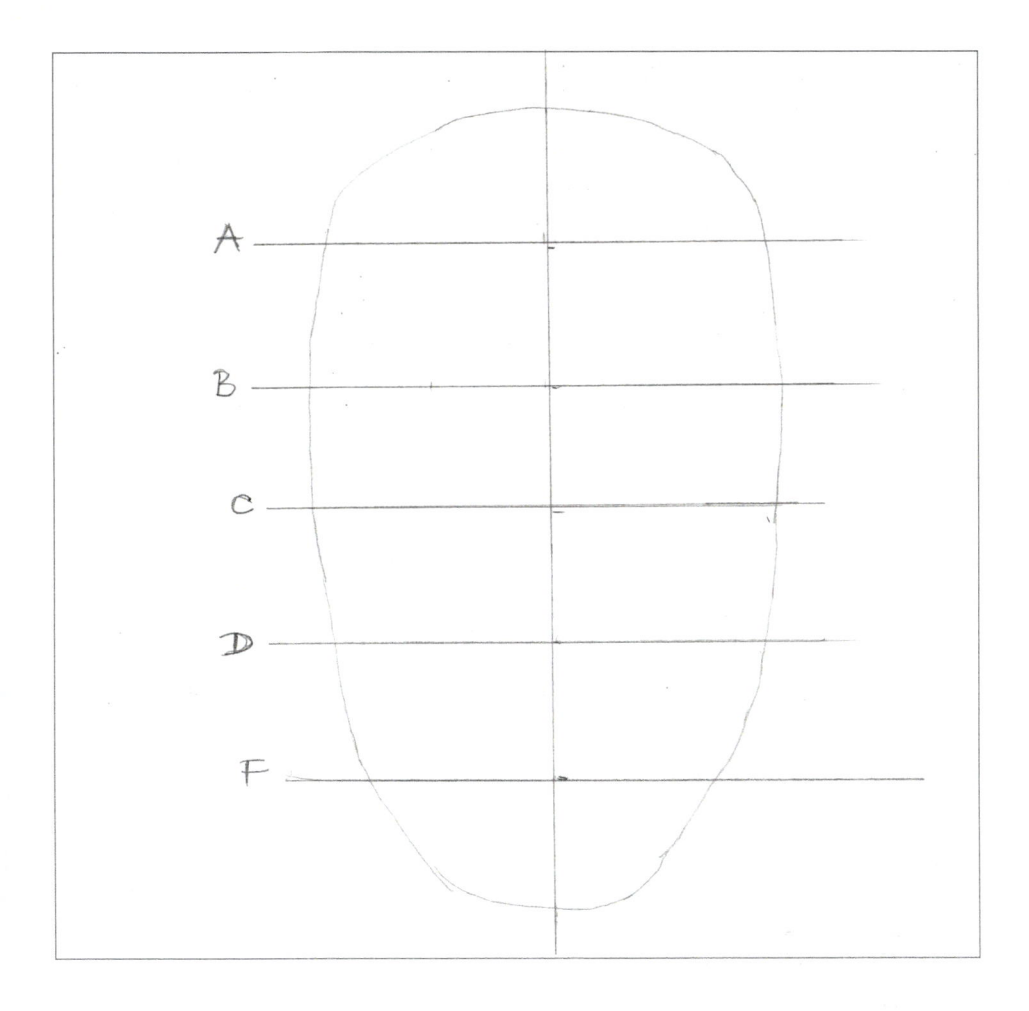

Then, divide each side of the top of the oval (above (B)), into thirds, shown here as (G) and (I) on the left, and (J) and (H) on the right.

Draw two small circles on the intersections of (A) and (G) lines, and (A) and (H) to indicate screws and bolts.
Using (A), (G), (J), (H), and (I) as guides, draw two squares on the left and right top of Iron Man's head, with a double line in the middle.
Below the top of his head, draw a square that passes

through (A), narrows as it approaches and ends at (B).

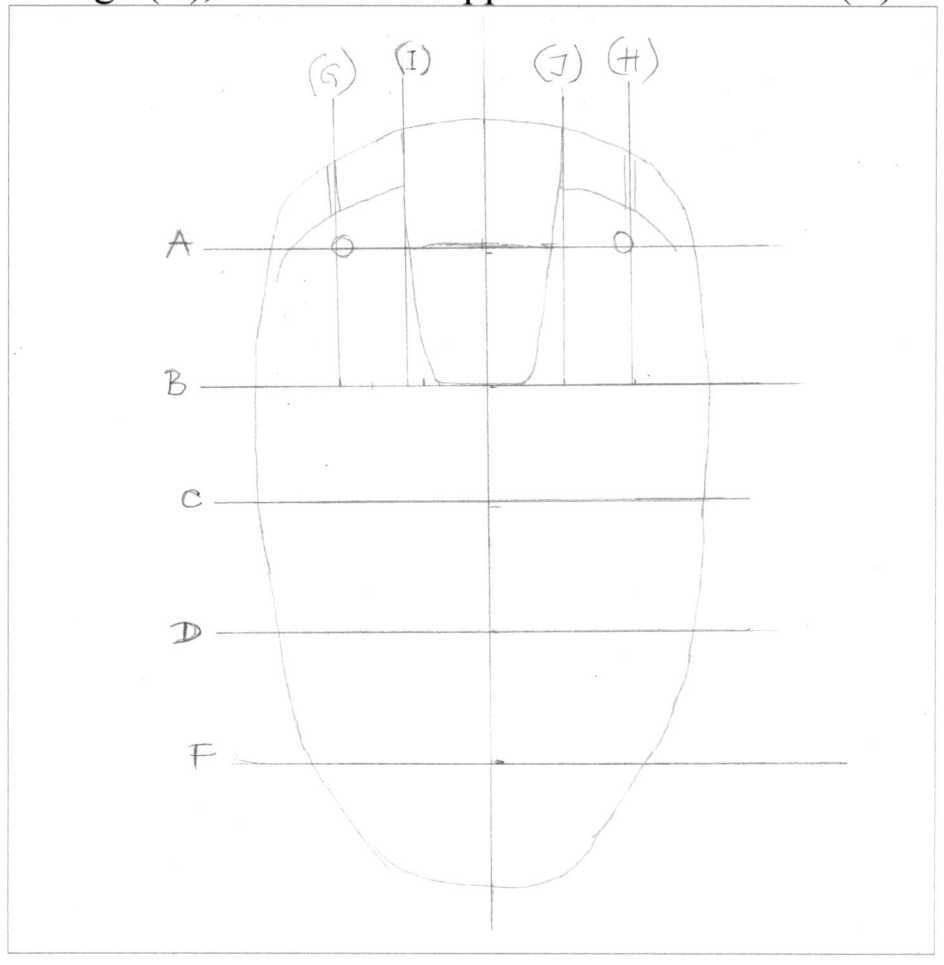

Now draw a long rectangle under (C), on each side of the vertical line. The eyes will be between (C) and (D) (you can see dashed line that I've drawn there). Draw another rectangle in each eye, and connect them with a double line which represents the gap between the face mask plates.

Draw lines between the outline of the Iron Man's helmet at (A) line and the outer angle of his eye. Do the same on the both sides.

Draw another line next to these, by his ears. Pay close attention to my main lines and don't press hard when sketching as you may need to erase a lot before you are happy with the outlines.

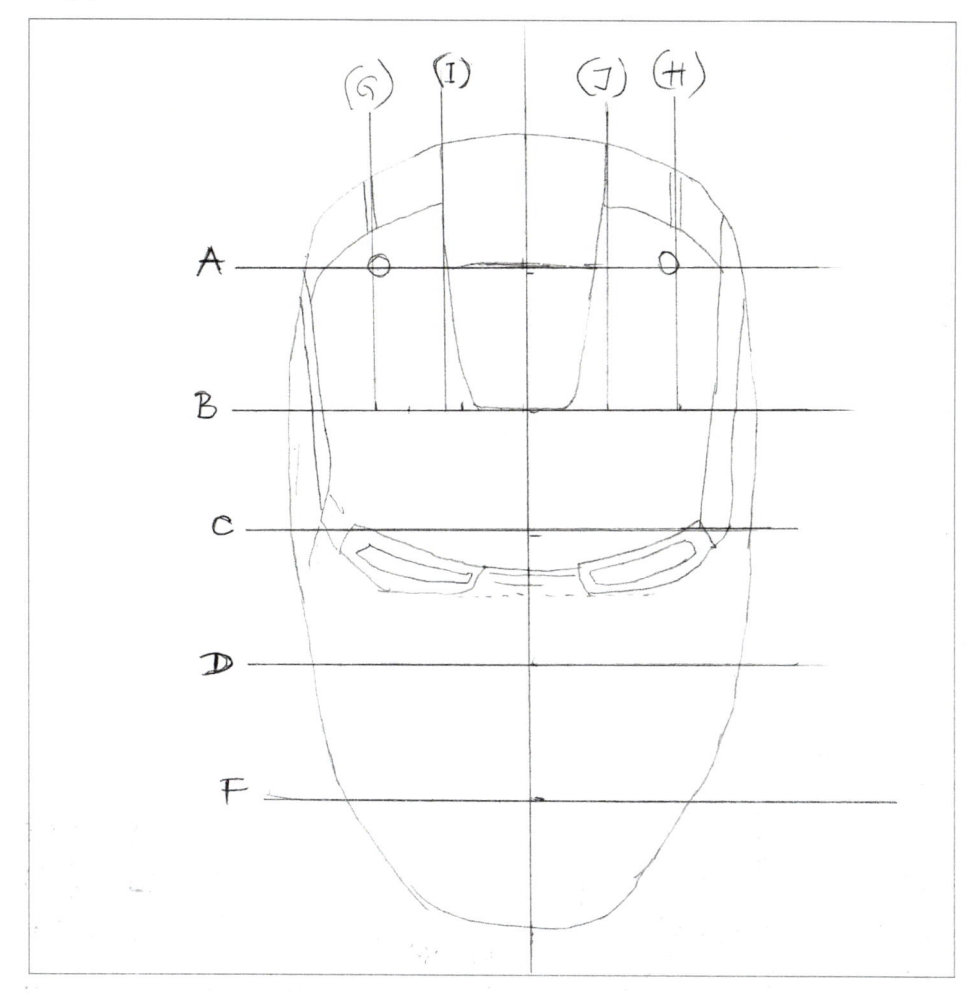

Draw a line a little above (F) and another a little below, followed by two double-lined V shapes for the gap of his mouth.

Draw a line from each of the V shapes, to line (C). Make them curve out toward the edges of the main oval to form his cheek plates. Draw a line following the shape of his mouth; somewhere between (F) and the bottom of his helmet. Connect them to his mouth by drawing two small lines.

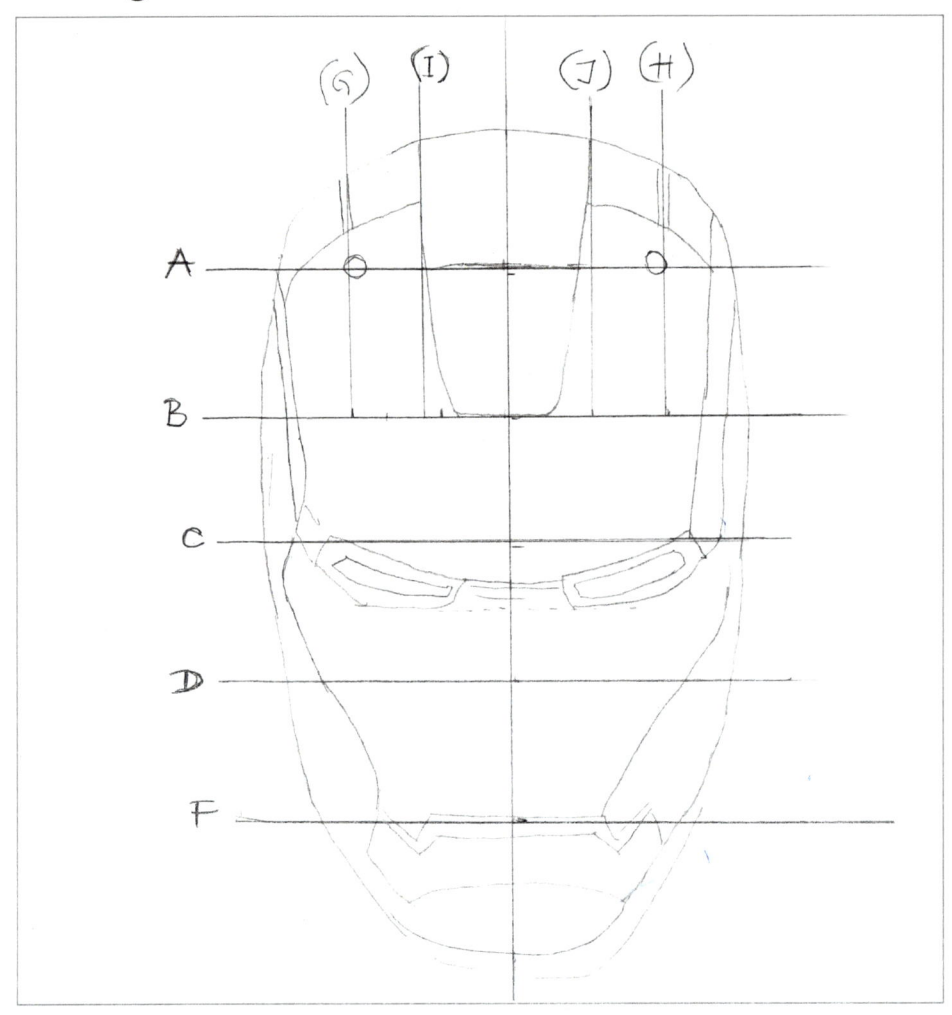

Finally, add part of his body if you want. The details will depend on which suit you draw. You can copy the

How to draw realistic movie characters with colored pencils

main lines from my sketch, or if you want to skip ahead and start coloring, you can print out the next image.

To start, darken the squares on top of his head. Mark all

How to draw realistic movie characters with colored pencils   Page 19

the black areas. These areas are actually red, but since they get no light, they appear black.

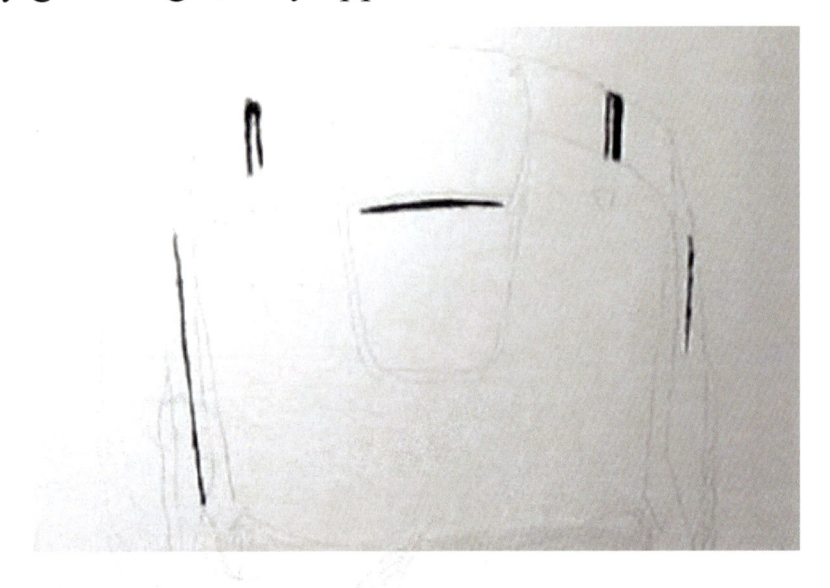

Start coloring the red parts of the top of his helmet using Crimson Red. You could use a similar red like Crimson Lake or, Scarlet Lake or Caran d'Ache's Crimson Alizan Hue. Whatever color you choose, use it as a basic color for the red iron parts.

If you don't like the color you've chosen, you can draw over the top in a more appropriate color or erase it with an electric eraser. The color won't be totally erased, but you still can color that area using other colored pencils. Of course, it's impossible to make white color after erasing the black and so on. You can avoid this by trying out the colors on another piece of paper before you apply them on your drawings.
If you want to achieve the smooth, even texture shown

in the next image, press really hard in a circular motion. Go over the same areas again and again until you've filled the tooth of the paper with color.

Continue to shape the red parts of the helmet with a well-sharpened black. If you are unsure and afraid of making a mistake, use a graphite pencil instead.

Graphite can be easily erased and when you are satisfied that everything is in the right place, you can go over it with black. Draw these main lines carefully, because they will determine the realism of your drawing.
The more accurate the main lines are, the more realistic your drawing will be.

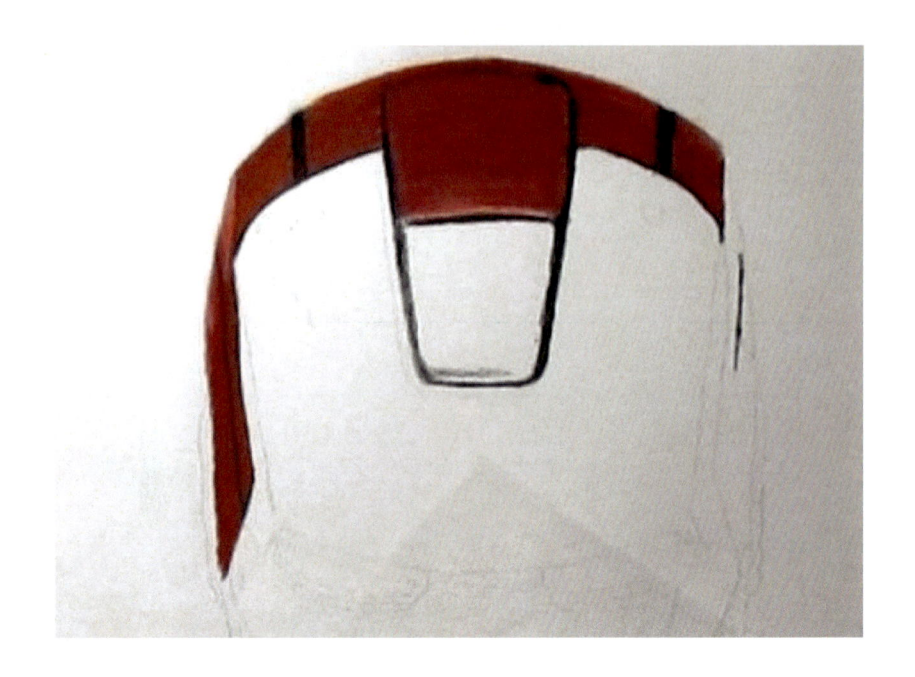

Fill in the red sheeting in the middle and on the right side. Go over the highlighted areas with white for a three-dimensional feeling.

Use Metallic Gold and Goldenrod by for the yellow parts of the helmet, and blend with French Greys.

Leave two small circles in these shapes white to indicate screws or bolts. The left side of the yellow sheeting should stay untouched, absolute white, since this area is affected by the light.

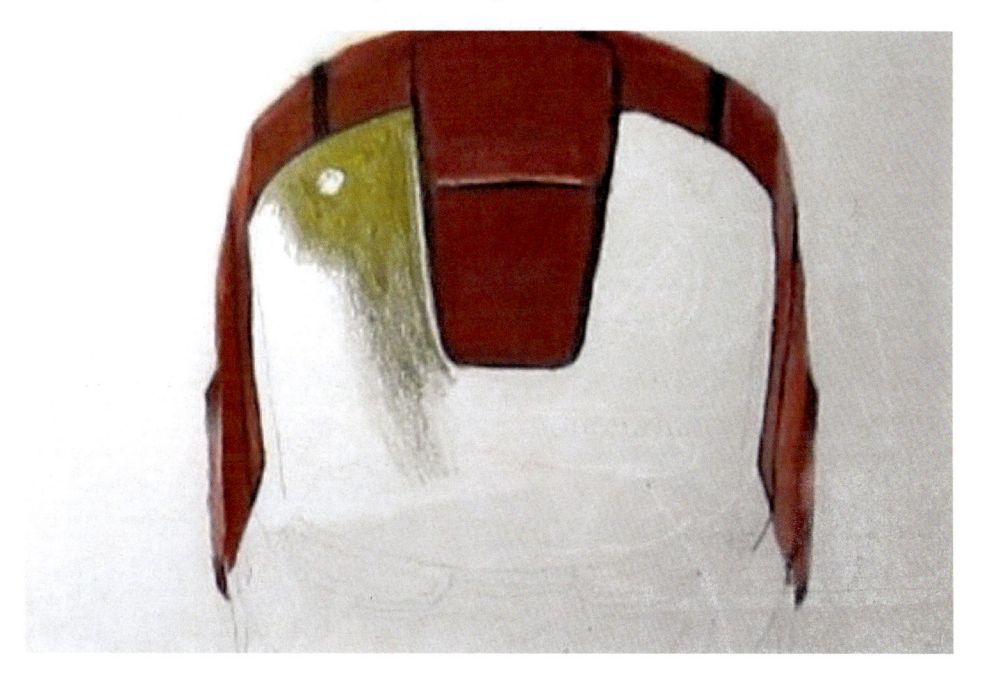

Blend the edge between the white and yellow area using a light grey colored pencil such as French Grey 10% or 20%.

I've also used some Cream to add more shine to the highlights. As you continue to color the "forehead" use more Cream and a brighter French Grey.

How to draw realistic movie characters with colored pencils

Grey pencils are excellent for achieving the shape of an object without putting too much color on the paper.

The next image shows the Prismacolor Premier grey palette (W = Warm Grey, F = French Grey, C = Cool Grey). You can even use them for human skin! They help progress your drawing easier than a simple grey pencil.

If you want to try them out, but don't want to spend a lot of money experimenting, just buy one (follow this link on Amazon and chose the color from the drop-down menu:
 https://www.amazon.com//dp/B000EVSCH8/

Try it out and buy the whole set if you find them good.

W 90%   W 70   W 50   W 30   W 20   W 10

F 90   F 70   F 50   F 30   F 20   F 10

C 90   C 70   C 50   C 30   C 20   C 10

Often the best way to blend colors is with a colorless blender or a colored pencil of a lighter hue. However, the colorless blender often darkens or lightens colors as well, which is why I recommend the light grey pencils for blending.

Move to the right side of the yellow part of the helmet and using the same pencils create a gradation from brown on the edge to shiny white in the middle.

The tiny part on the edge (between the yellow and red) should stay white.

Use French Grey 90% and 70% for the darkest parts of the yellow sheeting, and blend with Golden Rod and Cream.

You'll need a very sharp point to get the pencil tip down into the tooth of the paper. If you add to much color, you can lighten it with white pencils.

Before you apply white, use an electric eraser to erase the part that you find too colorful. This way you can still improve your colored drawing, unless you work with black and other dark colors which cannot be fully erased.

Now move to the left eye which is absolute white in the middle, surrounded by blue light drawn in Light Cerulean Blue. When you draw a shiny object, create a brighter area around it.

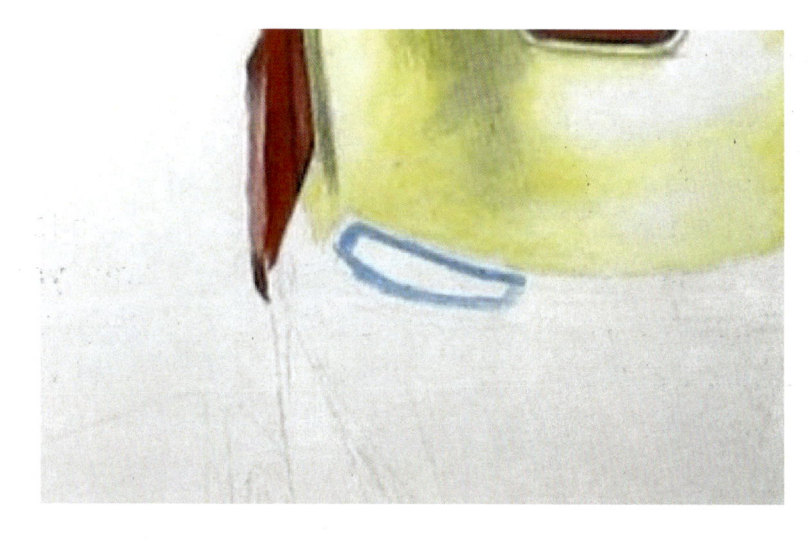

Draw the line between the forehead and eyes in Black. If you are unsure, draw it lightly with a graphite pencil (graphite pencil is easily erased). When you are sure everything is in the right place, go over it again with black.

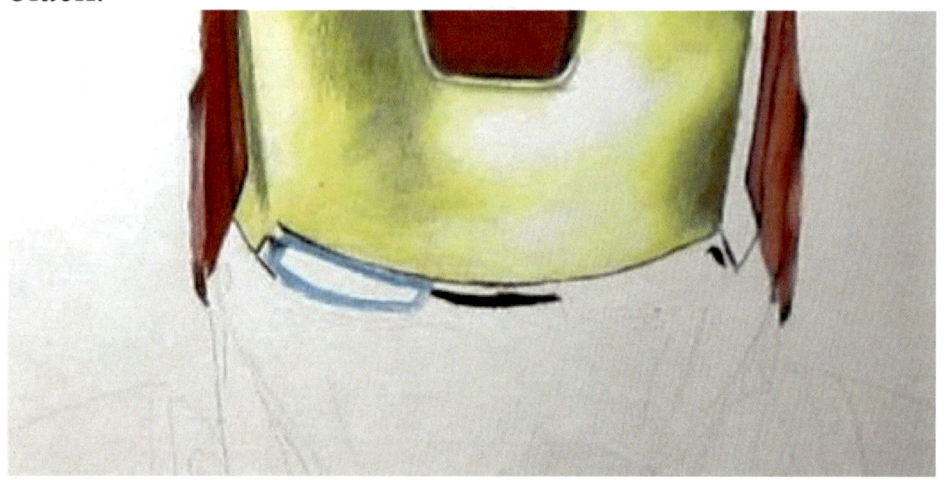

Continue with the right eye with the same blue as the left.

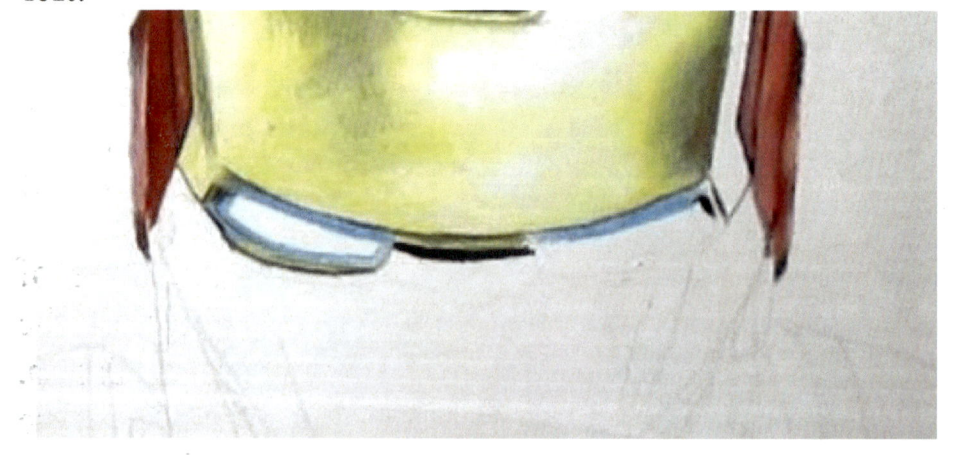

Now move to the area between the eyes and "mouth". It is important to leave both sides of the yellow sheeting untouched here as well. Draw only in the middle and create strong shadows between the highlighted and yellow parts. Use Golden Rod and Cream to create the basic color, then darken with French Greys 90% and 70% and white to lighten.

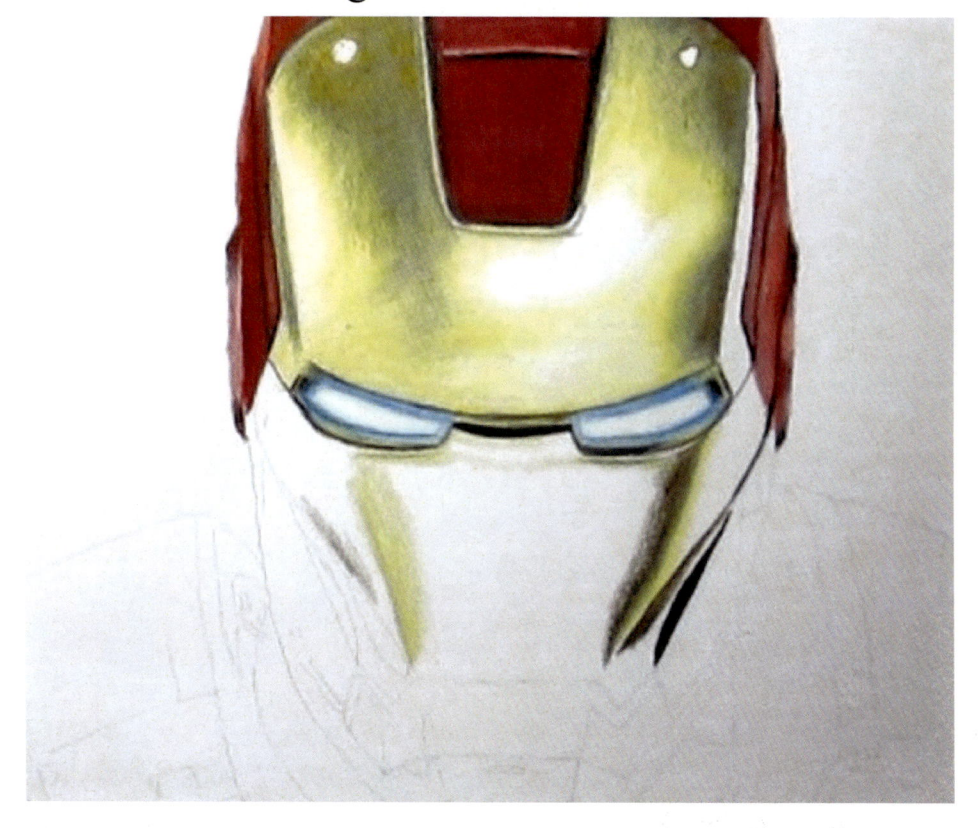

Fill the whole area with cream for the first layer of basic color. Then pile on layers of color to increase the intensity. Draw horizontally and vertically in Cream. This way you will get a smooth texture. Continue layering until you are completely satisfied with the smoothness of the texture.

Every step should be drawn carefully and with patience.

It's not easy to explain drawing techniques with words, which is why the step by step drawings are included. You can learn faster by seeing what I've done, and more easily remember what you've learned. In this step we laid down the basic color to darken and lighten in the following steps.

In the next image, you can see how I started darkening the parts that get less light. I used French Grey 70% because it is neutral and darkens without adding additional color to the Cream.

I don't use a wax colorless blender for blending textures like this, because it smudges and often changes the color. I use it mainly for drawings of animals.

You can see in the next image, you don't have to lighten anything, since light is coming from both sides, so it doesn't have to be absolute bright on the helmet front. Outline both sides with French Grey 90% and Black.

If you need to make a highlight more prominent, make the surrounding area darker. If your helmet doesn't seem bright enough, and you can't color the area brighter, shade around it with a darker nuance of the same color. Or use a Warm, Cool or French grey as they won't add color.

When shading around the area that you want to make prominent, touch the paper very lightly. As you move further from the highlight, use darker and darker nuances (check out the Prismacolor Premier grey palette on page 25).

When a gradual change is needed, start with a slight overlap in the middle, then progressively overlap each layer a little further. Once you acquire the gradient technique, you'll be able to draw anything easily, but this technique requires a lot of time and practice. Remember to make smooth gradients from light tones to mid tones and into the darker tones.

Here I started to draw the „jaw" after outlining the middle area of the helmet with a well-sharpened Black, then start drawing the "jaw" in Metallic Gold for the darkest areas of the yellow sheeting. This pencil is shiny, so it's absolutely appropriate for the metal texture. Keep your pencil sharp for nice clean edges. This area has a lot of details and will need more time and patience.

If you sharpen your pencil every couple of minutes, the tip will stay nice and fine which is vital for drawing details. Next add Cream in the middle of the "jaw" and shade with French Grey 30% where it needs to be slightly darker.

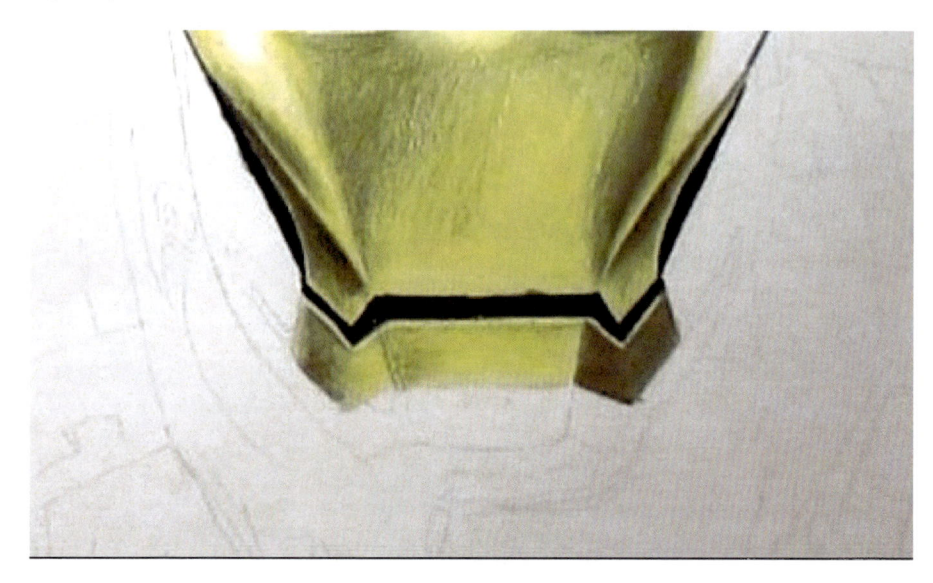

I would suggest you to watch me drawing Iron Man in my time-lapse video on YouTube:

https://youtu.be/3fwJP3cKQf8

 You learn best personally when you work as you watch someone else working instead of just pictures. However, the pictures do give an idea of how to use the techniques, and if you observe both - scanned steps in this book and time-lapse video - you can see the process of drawing and observe the things that I haven't mentioned. Drawing is a visual art and can hardly being explained only by words. Replay the parts of the video you haven't understood yet, more times. By watching, you can learn more and faster.

Next, add a bit of Canary Yellow all over the yellow metal, next to the highlights and shadows.

Next, use Crimson Lake for the shoulder plates. Draw the part between the shoulder and with Black since this area gets no light at all. Create highlights by burnishing the red areas with White.

Continue to add Crimson Red to the shoulder sheeting. To achieve an absolutely smooth texture, with no visible lines apply many layers of color in circles. The smaller and tighter the circles, the smoother the coverage. This is why you need a good quality, smooth, thick paper that can withstand many layers of hard pressed coloring. Thin paper will crumple and eventually tear with a lot of overlapping circles. Pressing Prismacolor Premier really hard on thick, smooth paper will achieve the smooth texture. If you can't get a smooth texture with the overlapping circles technique, draw over the same area with diagonal lines, from one corner to another and crosswise. Take a look at the next image to see how you should draw this area.

Layering is the most important technique for creating depth in your work. Cheap school style colored pencils will not give you the smooth, richly colored texture that you can achieve with the creamy, soft and highly pigmented Prismacolor Premier or Caran d'Ache Luminance pencils. Cheap pencils produce pale drawings.

As in any other field in your life; more expensive is usually better and cheap is not that good. It is worth paying a little extra to make your work easier and more pleasant. Even if you can't afford many good quality colored pencils, as mentioned in the "Tools" chapter, you can buy them individually.

The next image shows that you can achieve many nuances with the same pencil, by controlling how hard you press.

Plus, you can mix the colors. Yellow and blue create green, blue and red create purple, green and red create orange, and so on.

Go over the shoulder until you have filled the tooth of the paper. To create the highlights on the side and the top of the shoulder, blend the edges with White. Create the highlights on the red objects with White. Don't use pink even though that sounds logical, because it will be visible that you used different colored pencils. Use Dark Brown or Raspberry for the shadows, applying them over the basic red color. This way you will fill the tooth of the paper even more.
If you think it's too dark, you can erase with an electric eraser, and create lighter areas (though not absolute white anymore).

Now finish the helmet by coloring the side with the same red pencil.

You don't have to create shadows, only a tiny line for the highlight on the edge of the red sheeting with a well-sharpened White. The Prismacolor creaminess will leave the perfect, tiny trace on the red edge.

Use Black to create depth between the red and yellow sheets.

Now start to draw the rest of the shoulders in the same red. The initial sketch should be visible under the red colored pencil; you can strengthen the main, graphite lines with a well-sharpened Black colored pencil to keep the main lines visible.

How to draw realistic movie characters with colored pencils

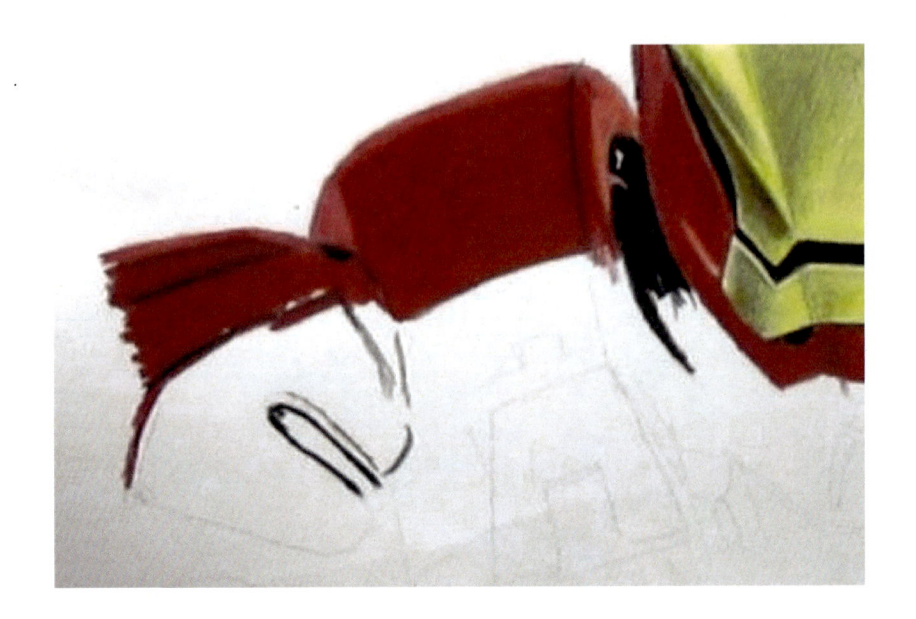

The same for the next step; strengthen the edges of the sheeting with Black, and go over the whole area in Red. As I mentioned, I chose Crimson Lake, because I found this color the most appropriate for his suit. Create tiny highlights with White.

The red area can stay even as it doesn't need shadows. If you cannot create absolutely bright highlights by applying white over red, consider where the highlights are found, and leave those tiny areas untouched. These parts will remain the natural color of paper and you just color around them.

If you're unsure, practice on another piece of paper until you are comfortable doing that. You can apply this technique in many situations. Or you could use a white ink gel pen to easily create tiny white lines over the colored pencils.

For product links go to my website:

http://jasminasusak.com/artsupplies/ to find the two tools that I use; a white ink gel pen and the Uni Posca fine white marker.

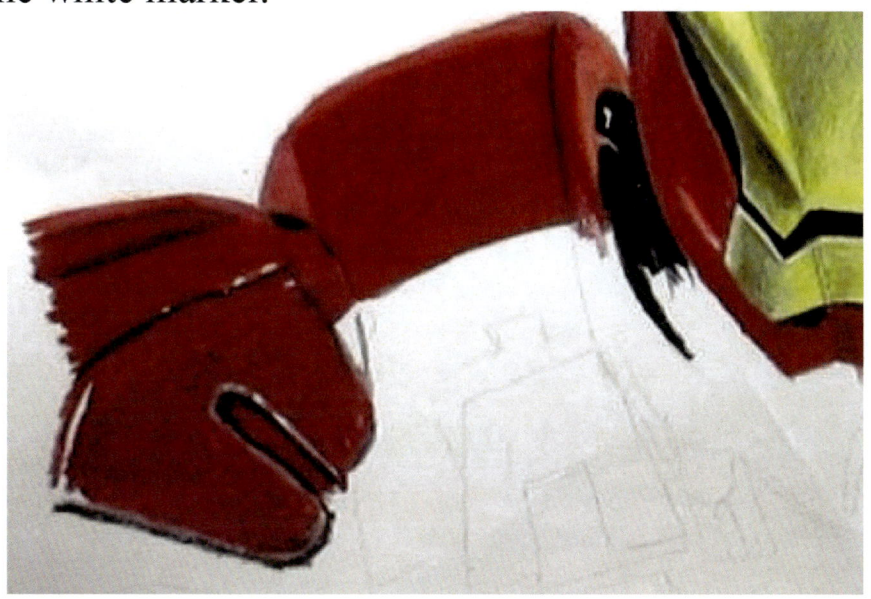

Next is the silver clamp on his chest in Silver. Compare this image with the previous to better understand what I have done.

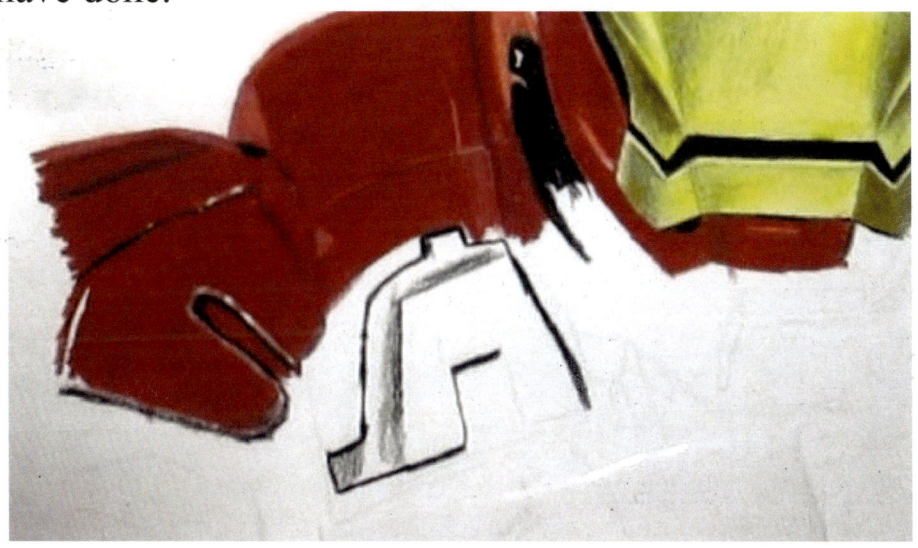

The clamp has shadows and highlights in Cool Grey. Referring back to the Prismacolor Premier grey palette on page 25, you can see that Cool Grey is the most similar to silver. You could use Warm Grey, but French Grey is not a good match for this area.

The clamp has a bend in it which divides it into two area. The top is a little shaded by the way Iron Man is standing, and the bottom seems much brighter because it gets more light.

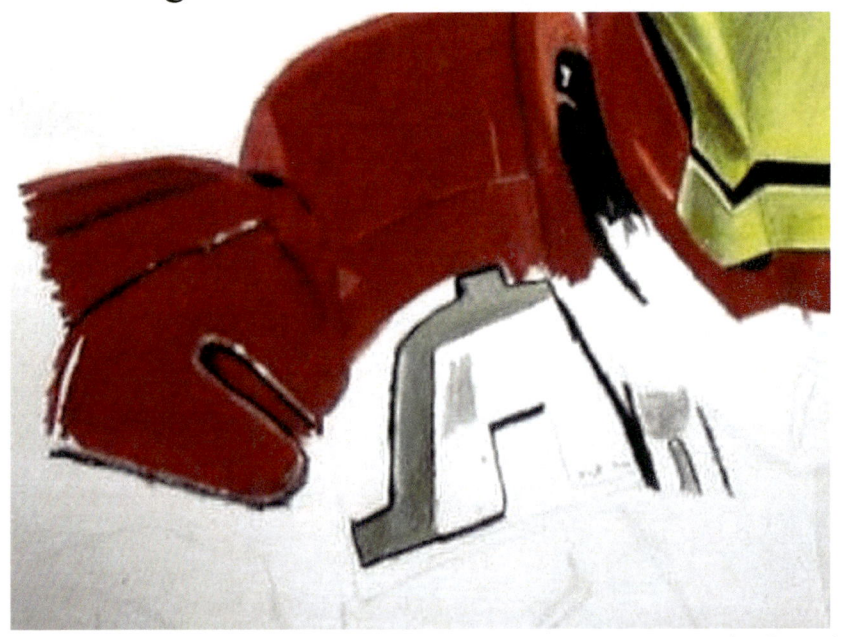

Use Silver with a layer of Cool Grey 20% over it for the brighter side, then a well-sharpened Black to create the gaps between the silver and red metal areas. Underline the silver clamp strongly so it appears to stand off the paper.

Use a well-sharpened white pencil to create the tiny highlights on the edges of the red sheeting. Press really hard with the White to erase the red color.

How to draw realistic movie characters with colored pencils

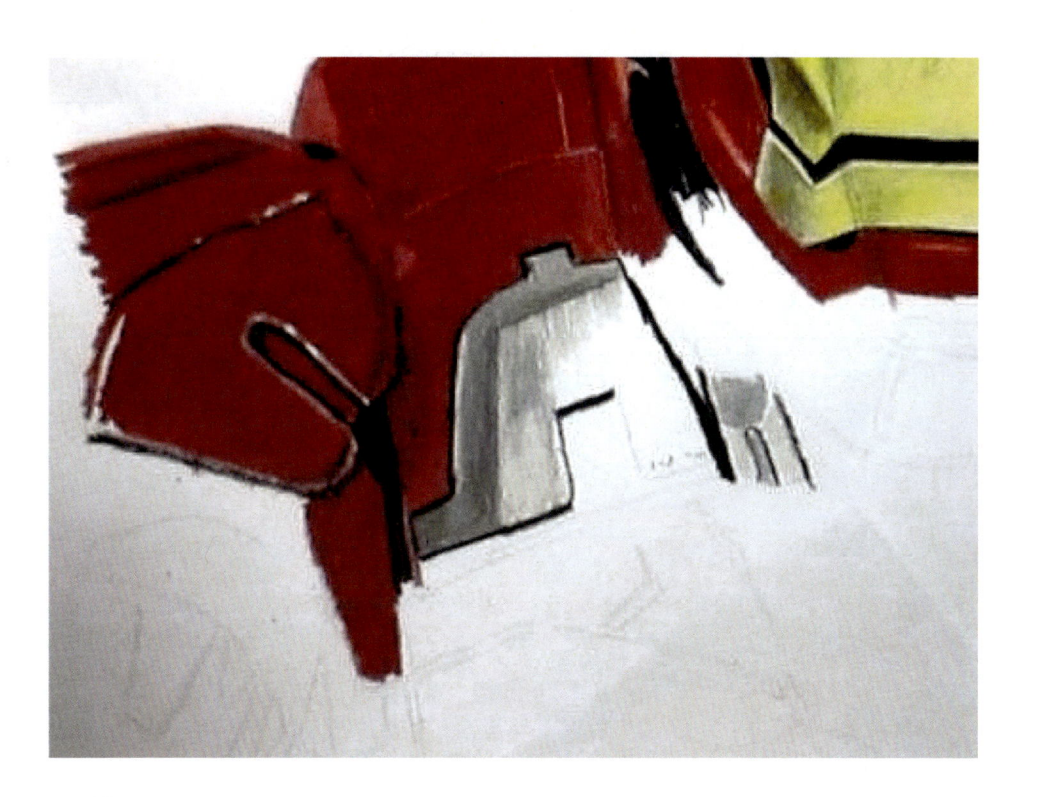

With the shoulder part of clamp complete, fill the rest of the shoulder in with Crimson Red, and create a wide gap between chest and arm in Black colored. Since his chest is curvy, the black and red cannot just be drawn by one another; they have to flow into each other to achieve a gradation between the colors. You can color this with Black Raspberry or Dark Brown.

A wax colorless blender often changes the colors and fluffs the texture, so for the areas like this where you need it smooth, I recommend blending with colored pencils instead.

Finish the red area of his arm and move on to the rest of the chest.

Draw the red metal sheeting between the previously drawn red and yellow (which you will draw later). Color the whole area in Crimson Lake, or the red nuance you started with.

Add a tiny shadow under the previously drawn red sheeting using Dark Brown or Black. Create the tiny silver area with the Silver. Try to keep them all separated by the tiny black lines.

Next, underline the silver clamp with red, and then underline in black to make it appear closed. Create small highlights over the red, in White. Draw the area between the neck and silver clump with Crimson Red and shade it with Dark umber and Black raspberry.

Now you can move onto the right shoulder. This tutorial doesn't include the full arm on the right side, but you can add it if you want to make the full body.

For this area, use the same, Crimson Lake pencil, and create shadows with Dark Umber, Dark Brown and White, with highlights in White.

You don't have to create a bright edge over this shoulder, just go over it with white to make it look brighter than the rest of the red sheeting.

The next step is about creating his "neck". Using Crimson Lake, color the whole area and create the sheeting edges by drawing a tiny White line along it.

Then create the shadows in Dark Brown. To make it appear smooth, go over it again with Dark Brown, and again with Crimson Lake. If you think that your shadowed area is still not smooth enough, repeat one more time with Dark Brown and Crimson Red layers. The more layers you create, the smoother the texture will be. This is why it isn't enough to just draw something in only one colored pencil.

Now draw the clamp on the right side with Silver as the main color. Create highlights by pressing lightly with Silver and blending with white. Or you could leave the white color of the paper untouched. Use Cool Grey 50% and 70% for the silver shadows. While the clamp should be as smooth as possible, tiny lines or imperfections can represent scratches on the metal sheeting. Outline the whole clamp with well-sharpened Black.

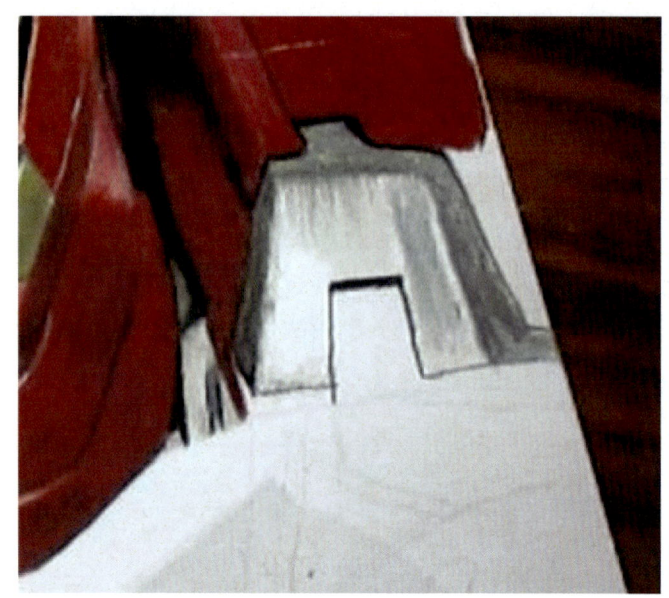

Next, draw the red area around the clamp, trying not to go over the silver area. If necessary, you can go over the black outline, but any red on the silver will be more difficult to correct. Continue to use Crimson Lake color, highlight with White, and underline in Black to separate this part from the sheeting on his chest.

How to draw realistic movie characters with colored pencils   Page 48

Now we can add the details under his neck, and start drawing his chest. His chest is mostly red sheeting, so draw tiny lines to separate the sheeting.

If you drew your initial sketch correctly, you just have to strengthen your initial lines and fill in the rest with Crimson Lake.

The black lines of your drawing will still be visible under the red, so you can see where to add shadows and highlights. Use Cool Grey 30% for the tiny metal part in the middle of his chest, under his neck. Analyze my next image to see which part I mean and what exactly I have drawn.

Move to the right side and draw the red sheeting under the clamp. Fill the gap between the sheets with Black. Go over the edges of the Red with White to make the sheeting seem to stand off of the gap.

Since I'm right handed, I always finish the areas on the left before I start on the right to avoid smudging, if you are the same, move to the left arm to finish it. If you are left handed, start areas on the right before you move to the left and hold your hand on a clean piece of paper of nylon.

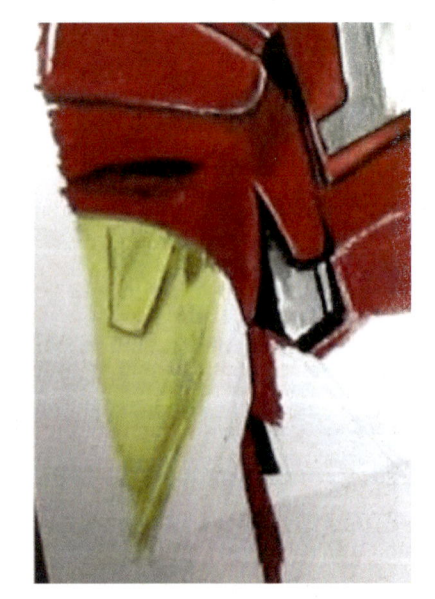

Use Cream and Metallic Gold for the yellow sheeting on his arm, with French Grey 90% and 70% for the shadows and White for the highlights. For the inner arm, use Crimson Lake, and since this area gets less light, use Dark Umber over the top. Draw tiny silver details on the left side of his chest, and use Black to create strong shadow around them.

Next, start to draw the large, red chest plates with Crimson Lake. There will be strong highlights in this area so leave them untouched and color around them for now.

In the next image, you can see that the metal already appears shiny, but you will blend it more later. As mentioned earlier, use circles and diagonal strokes to create the smooth texture. Add a layer of Crimson Red and another of Crimson Lake; press really hard to fill the tooth of the paper. If you use Prismacolor Premier, your work can be much easier since these colored pencils are creamy and easy to spread.

Next, blend the edges between the red and untouched white areas with White, and you could also go over the highlights with White.

If you exaggerate and bring too much red over the highlights, you can easily eliminate it with electric eraser and recolor with white, pressing hard, making multiple layers until you achieve the white color.

The best solution is to make gradation between red and white. It doesn't have to be perfect, just to avoid red and white flowing directly into each other.

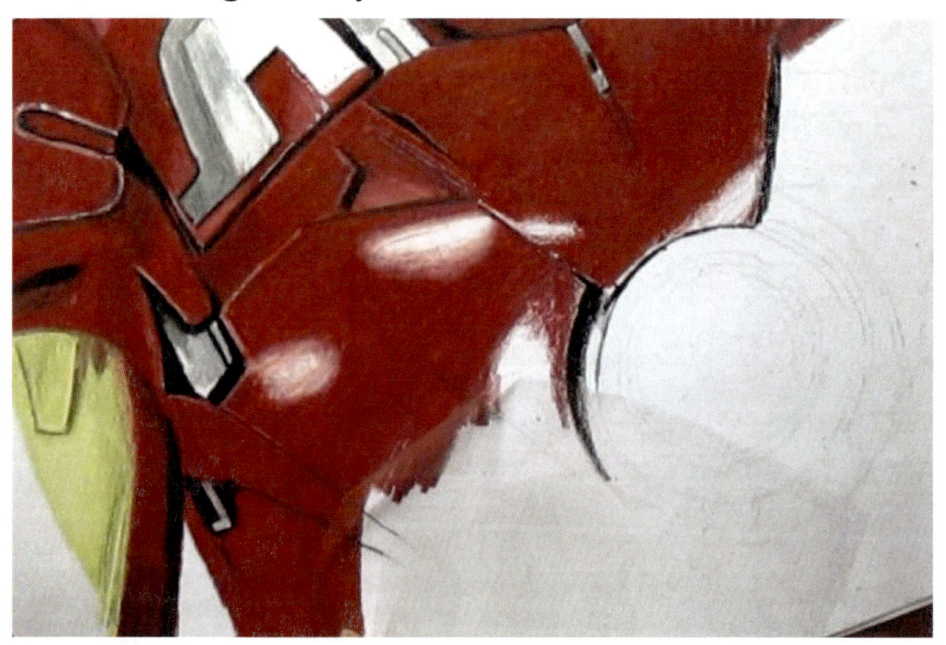

Color the rest of the left lower chest. There is only one highlighted part, the rest should be darker.

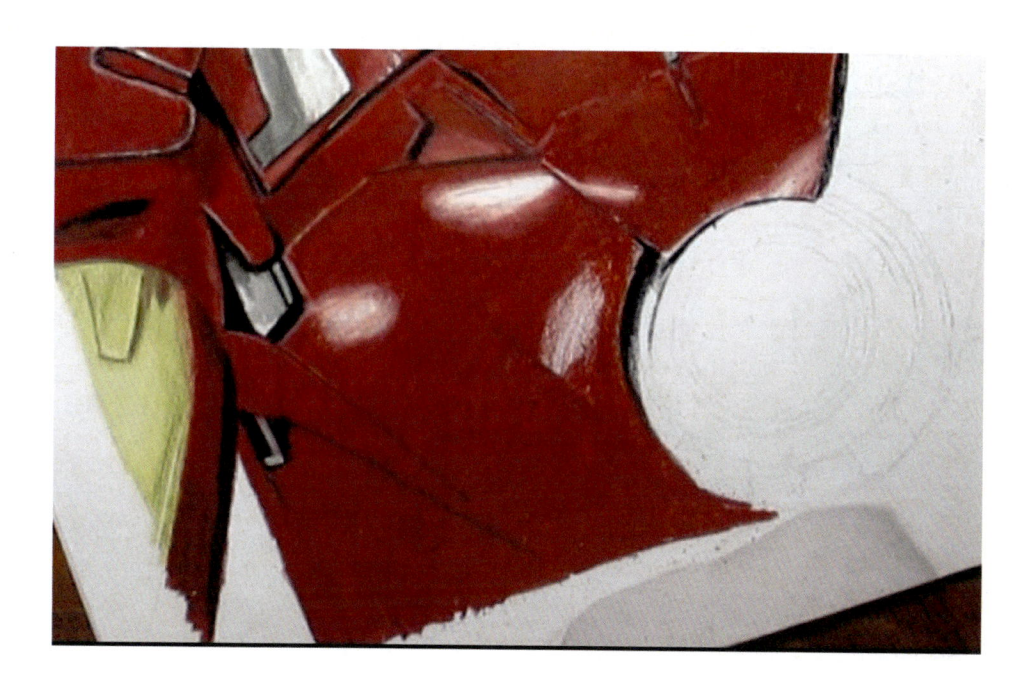

Blend it all with Crimson Red, layering again with Crimson Lake to make it look smooth. Draw the shadowed parts in Dark Umber, going over the previously drawn red areas on the left side waist sheeting. If the area turns out too dark, go over it with Crimson Lake to lighten it.

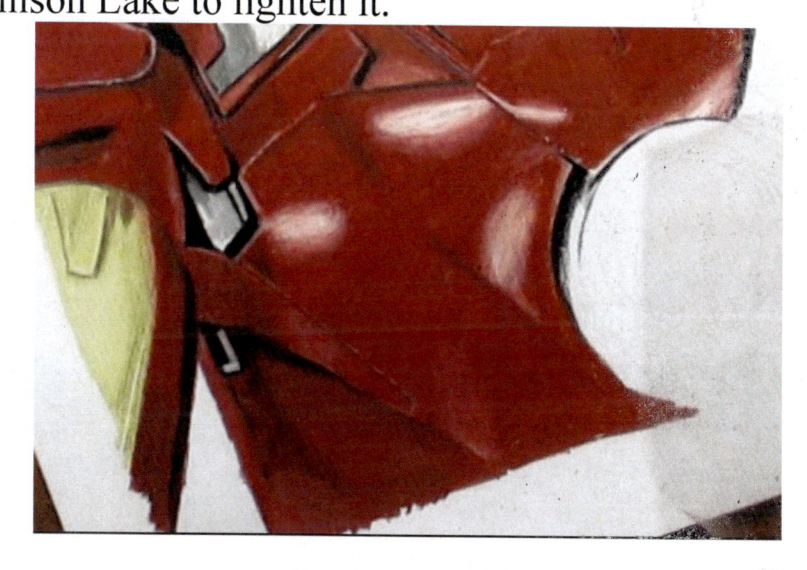

Now move to the right side and do the same; color everything except the highlights. Create the gaps between the sheets with Black.

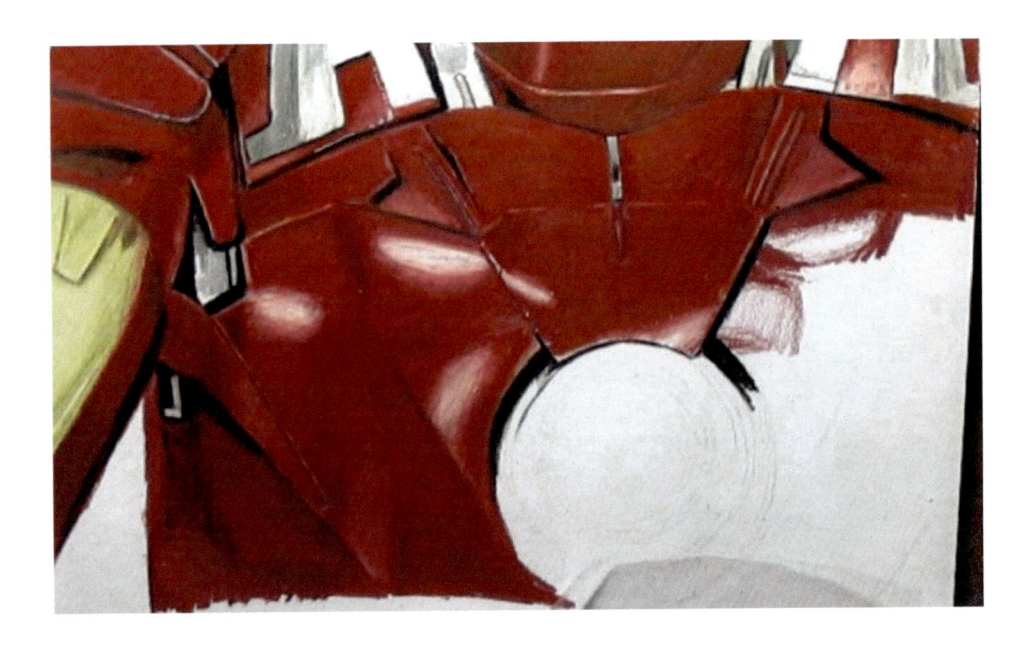

If you created the lines before applying the red, you can go over them again with black. While you are drawing, the black areas will get dusty and lose contrast. Always create one last layer over the darkest parts, though you could leave this to the end of the drawing. Again, create the first layer with Crimson Lake, the second with Crimson Red, and third with Crimson Lake.

Before you finish the right side of his chest, draw the lamp in the middle of his chest. As the lamp appears to be turned on, you have to create a bright area around it, that looks shiny. Strengthen the main lines around the area the blue circle will go.

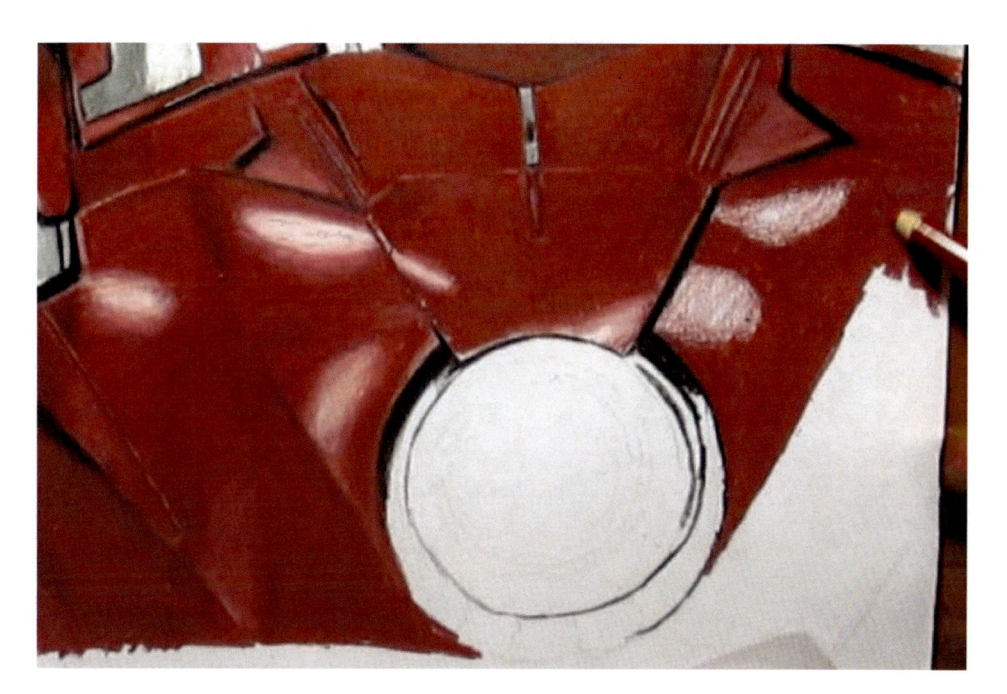

Blend the highlights over the previously drawn red areas with White.

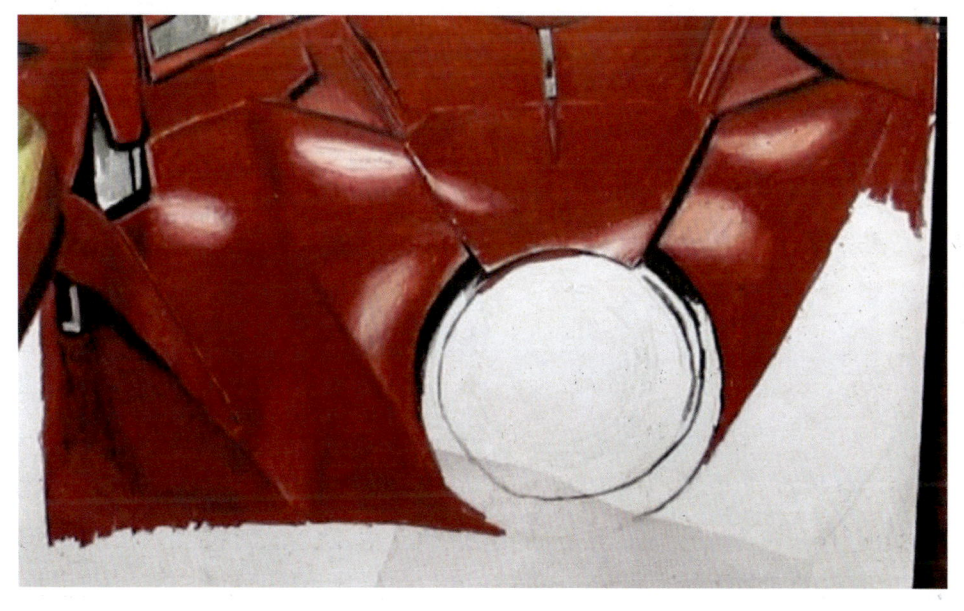

You can see the blue circle is located near the center of the hole left for the lamp. Draw it in Light Cerulean

How to draw realistic movie characters with colored pencils   Page 55

Blue, and blend with White to make it look bright.

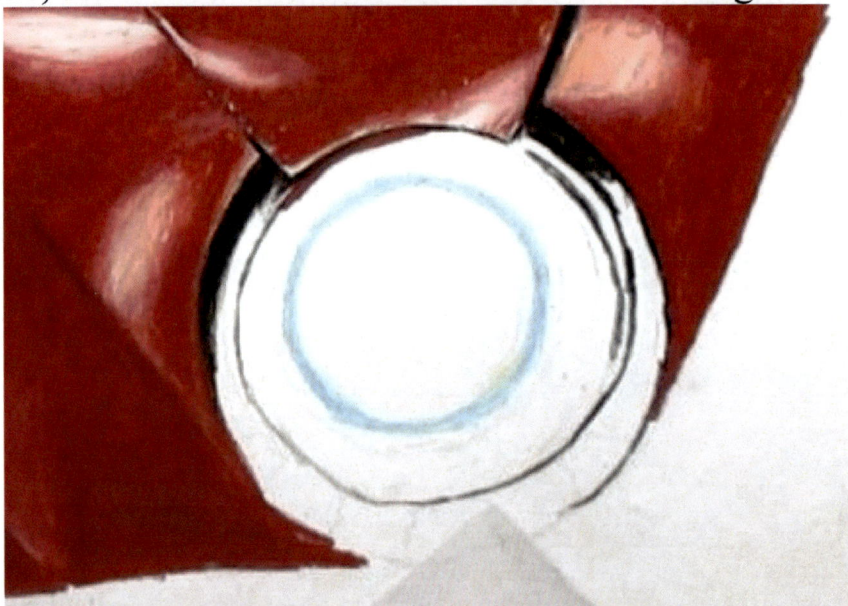

Draw a tiny yellow circle just inside the blue circle, and blend with white. The inner area of the circle stays absolute white, so you don't have to touch it at all.

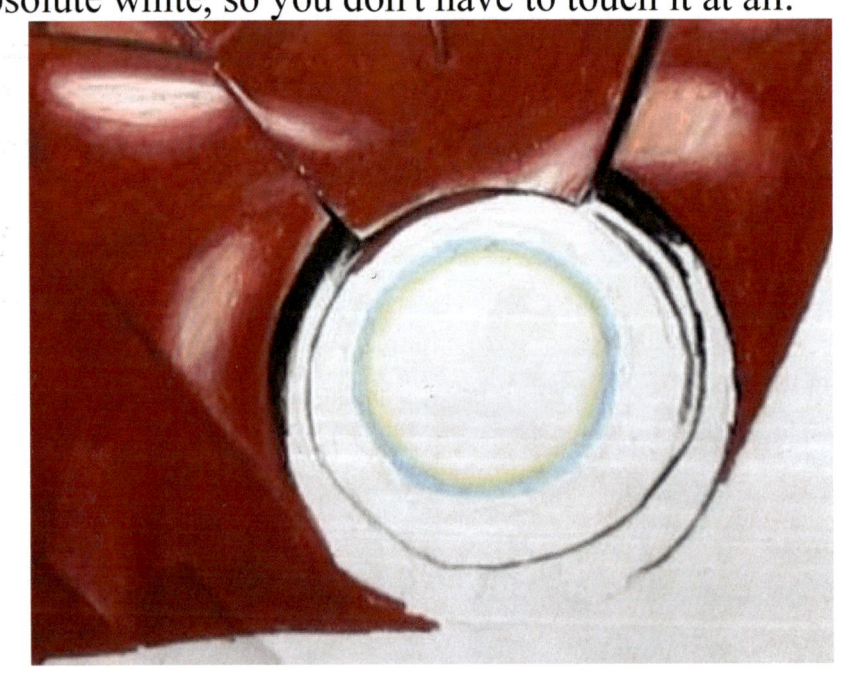

How to draw realistic movie characters with colored pencils

Draw around blue circle in Crimson Lake and Crimson Red, making it as smooth as possible.

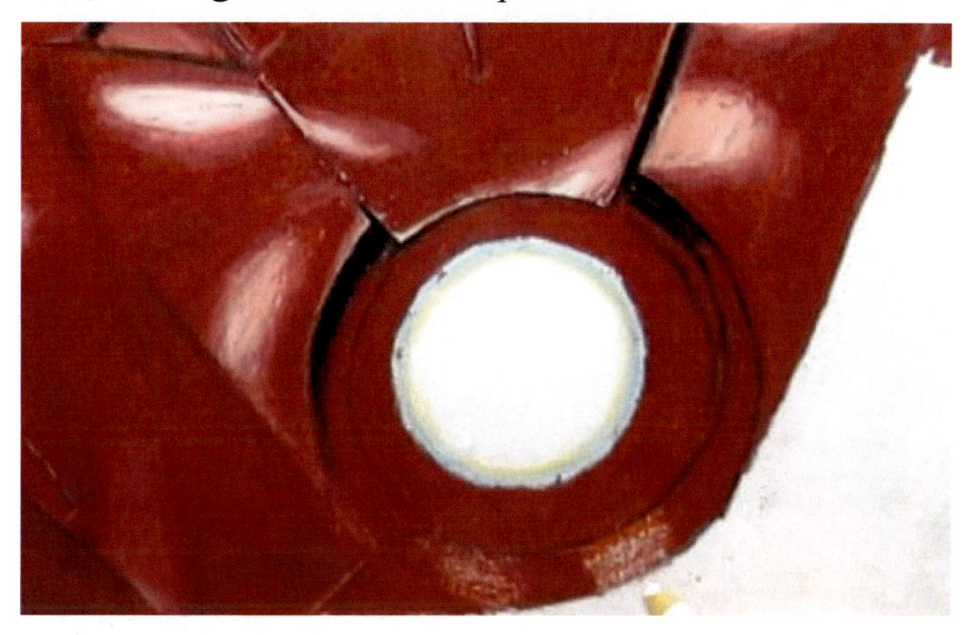

Blend the red area around the blue circle in White, and as you move away from the lamp and the blue circle, blend less and less. This makes the area next to the lamp look much brighter and as if the lamp is turned on.

Step back from your drawing to check the result. Often you won't notice mistakes when looking at the drawing closely all the time.

You can also change your perspective by looking at your drawing in a mirror; you will see mistakes you haven't noticed before. Using a mirror is particularly useful when drawing something symmetrical, for example, a bottle or ball.

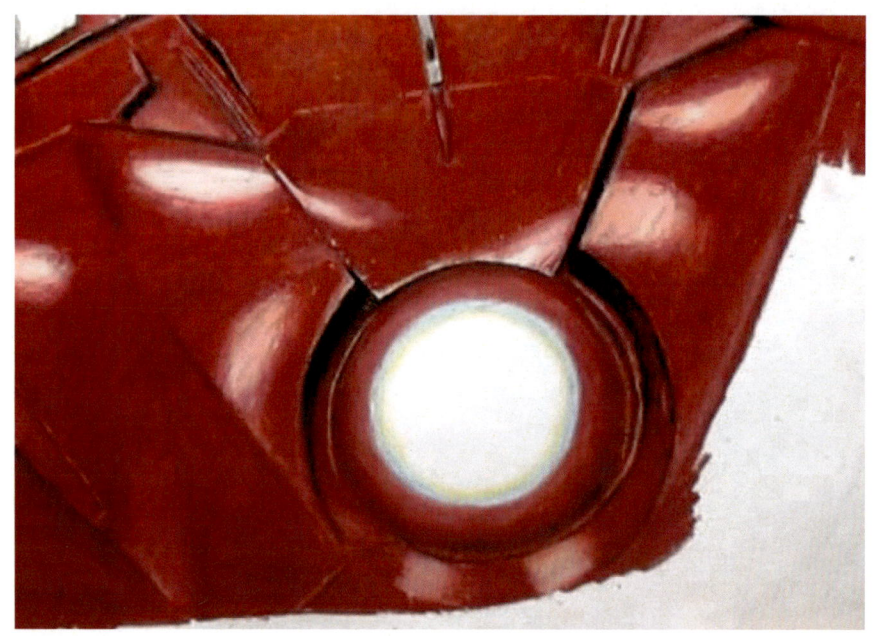

Now finish the rest of the right side of his chest using the same pencils.

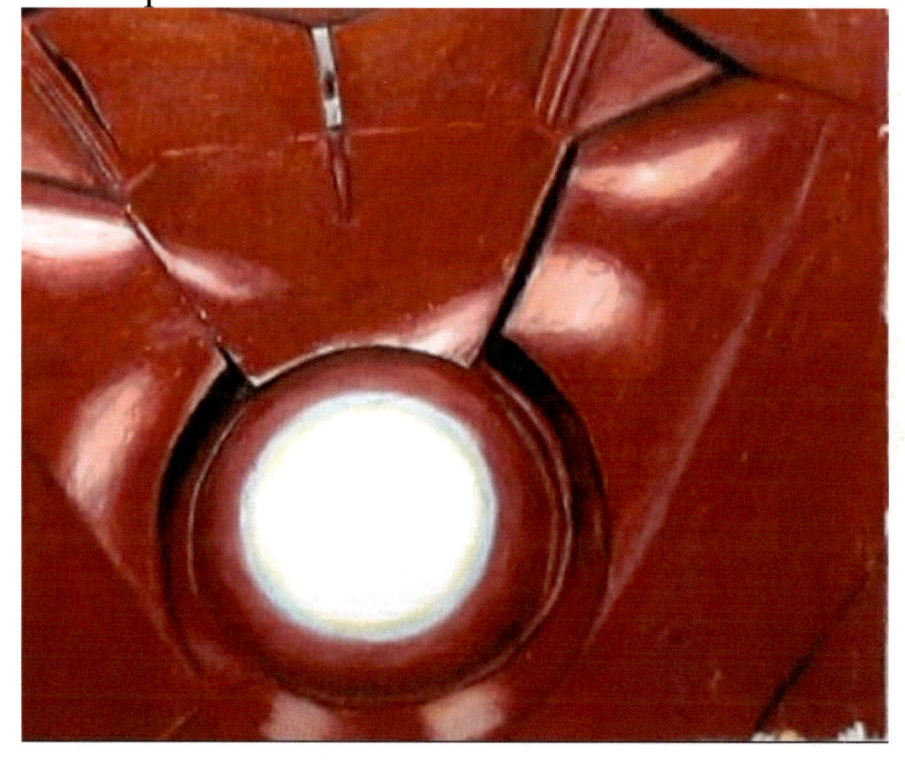

How to draw realistic movie characters with colored pencils   Page 58

Final, scanned drawing:

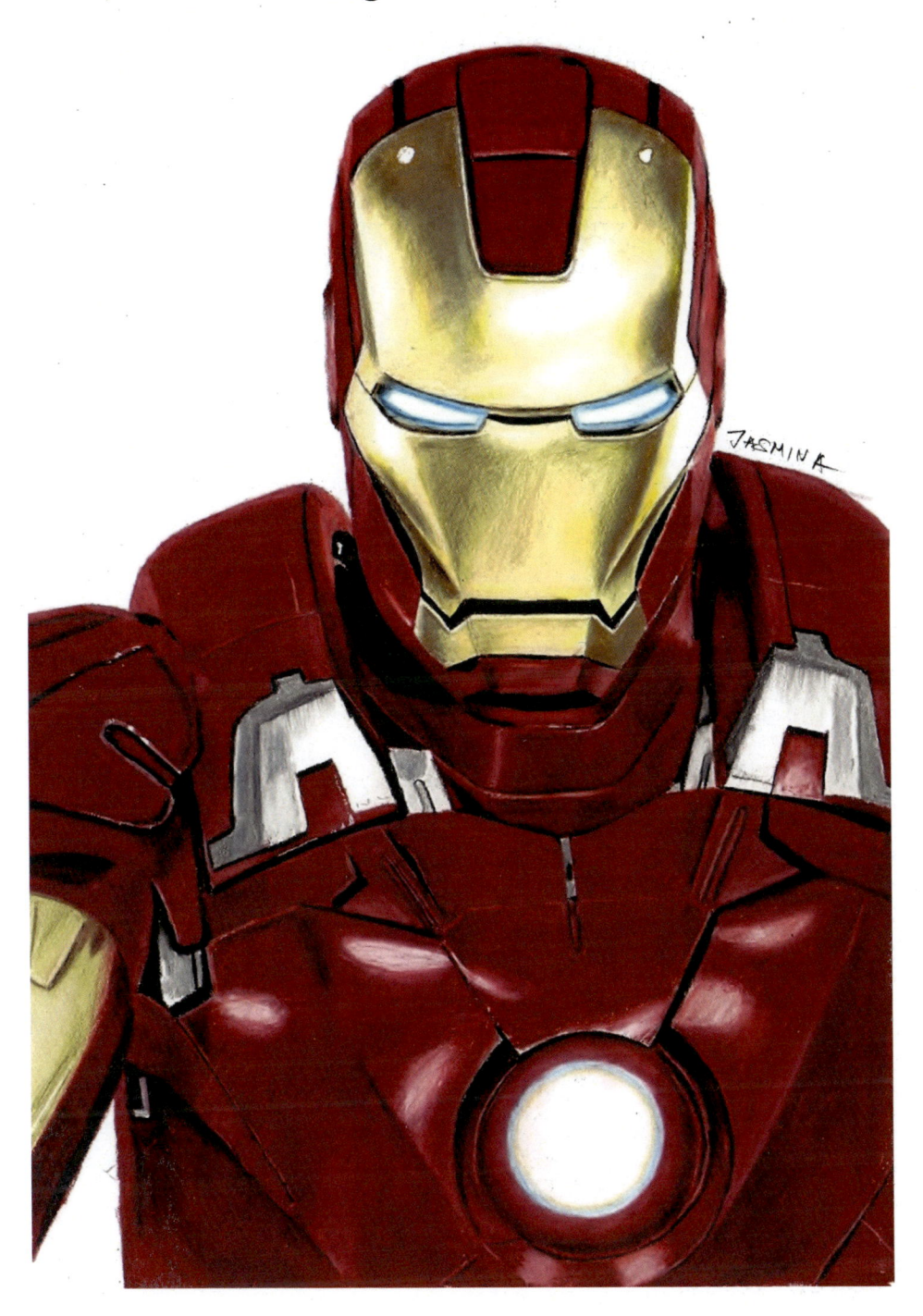

How to draw realistic movie characters with colored pencils Page 59

Iron Man, commissioned work
Colored pencils and graphite, 8" x 11"

Deadpool

First draw an oval, and divide it in half vertically with line (A), and horizontally with line (B).

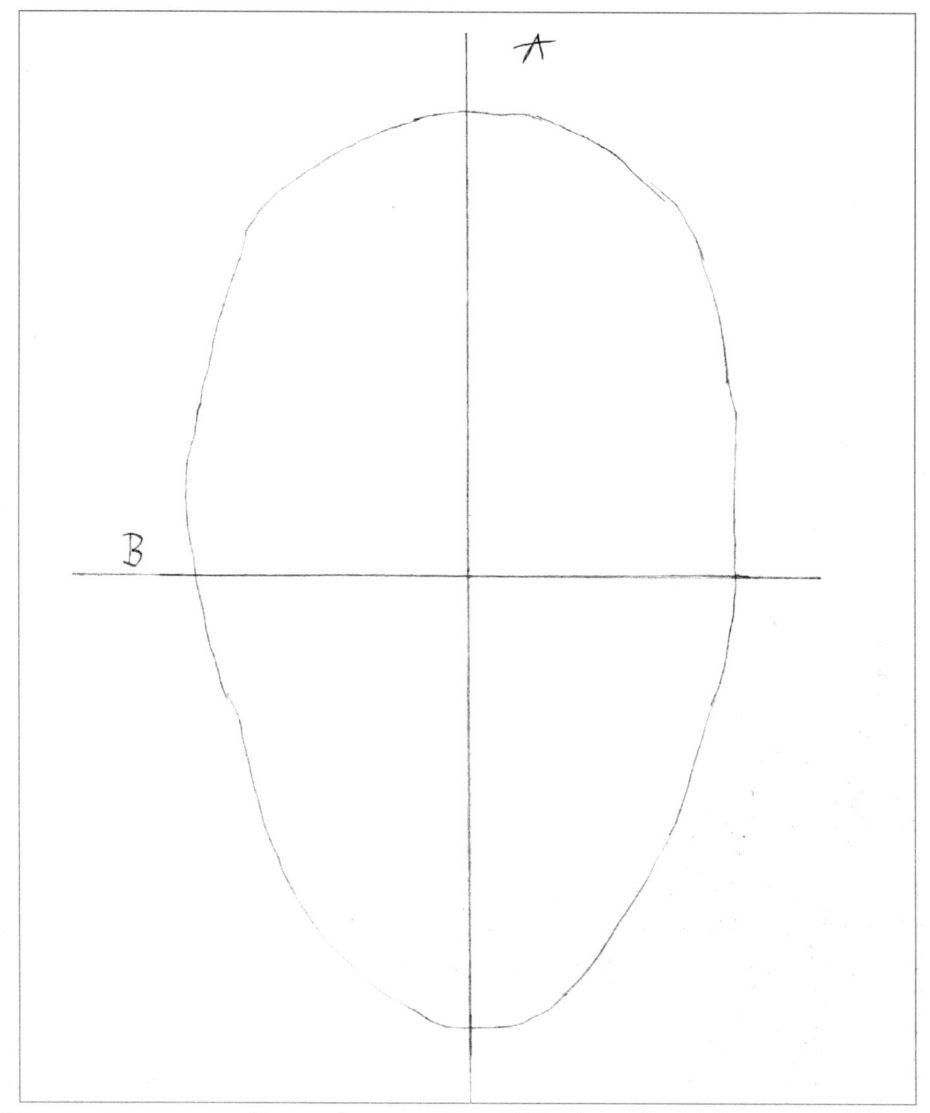

Draw two small ovals on the (B) line for his eyes. They don't have to be exactly over the line, nor do they have

How to draw realistic movie characters with colored pencils

to be equal. The distance between them should be the width of an eye.

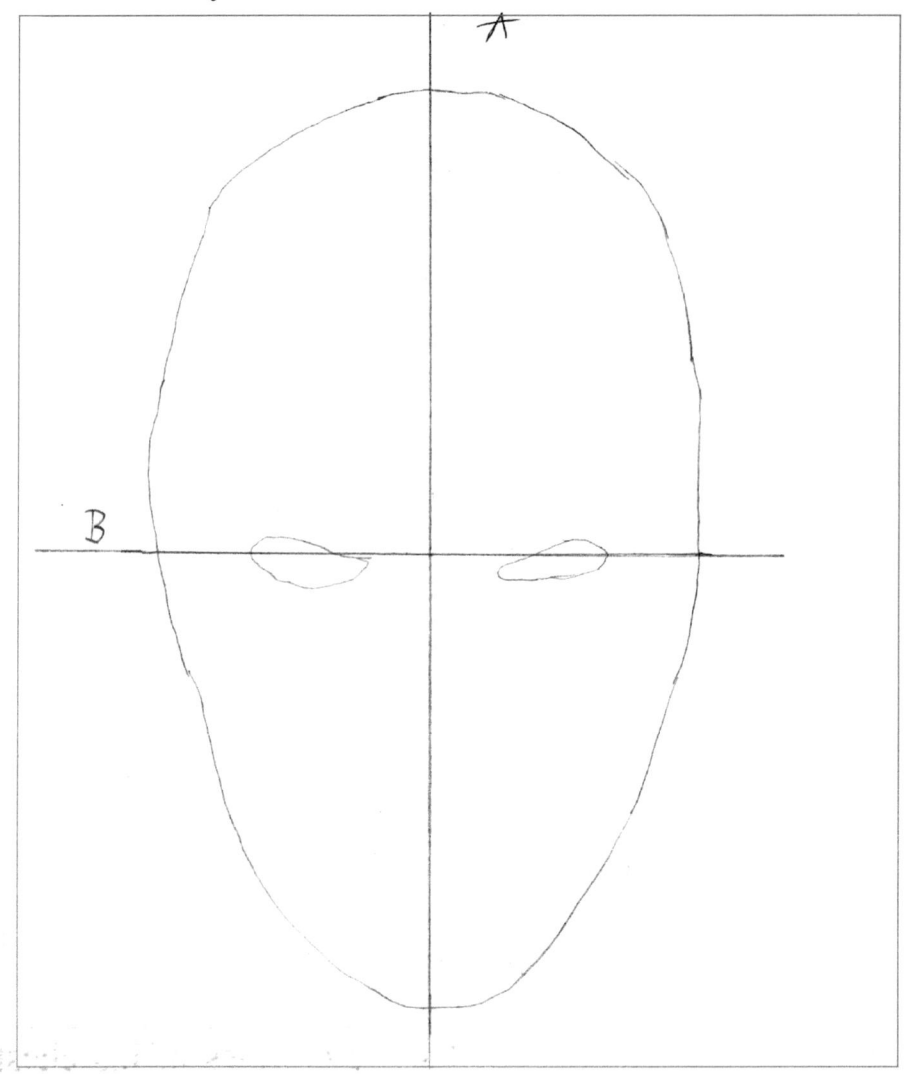

Next draw the mask's pattern. Deadpool's mask is very simple, consisting of an oval-like shape surrounding each eye. Draw double stiches around the main oval line. Analyze the next image to see where to draw them. Create the lines around his eyes to indicate the curves

How to draw realistic movie characters with colored pencils

of the black leather.

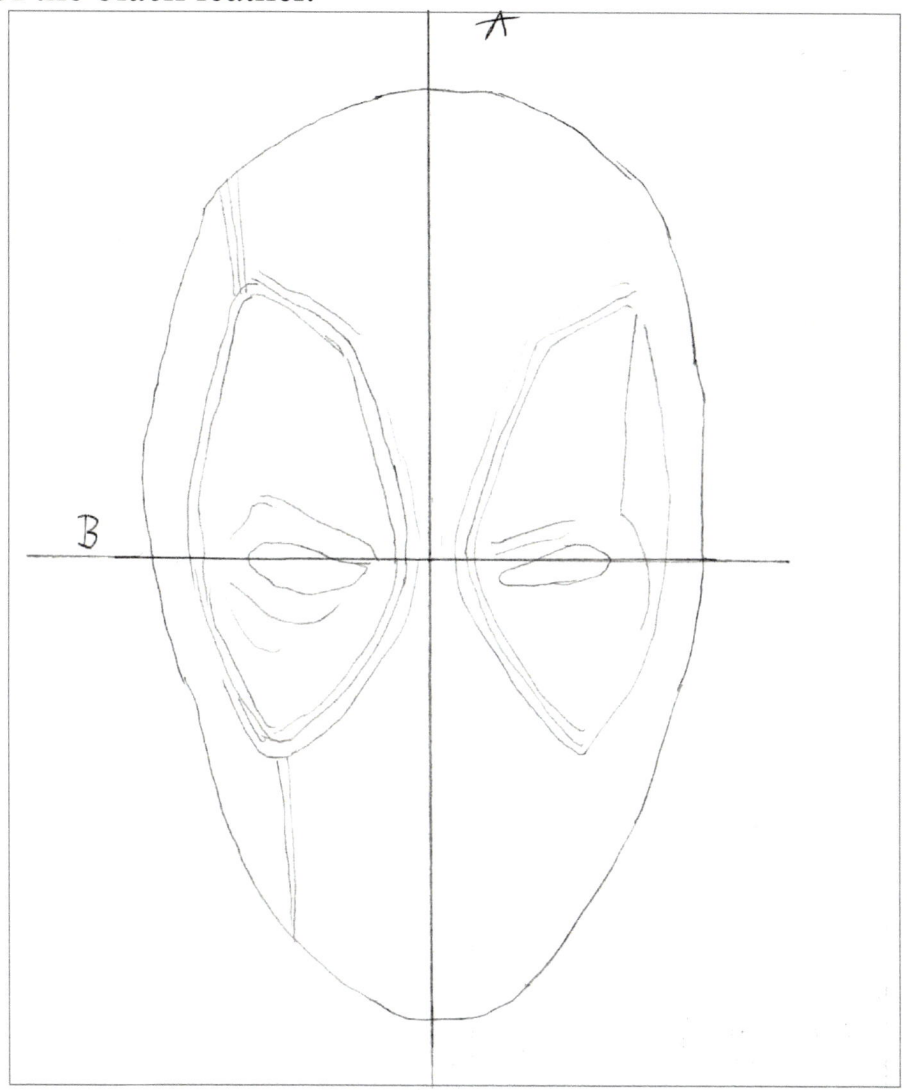

Add his sword handles and some outlines of his chest. In the next image, you can see my main lines, but you could draw the handles in different places, or skip them altogether if you want to draw just his head. You can add more details after finishing the head. If you want to make the same drawing, thoughtfully analyze the image and try to recreate the outlines. If your sketch is not the same, or not proportional, don't worry. It doesn't have to be perfect, or like a photo. You will achieve more proportional drawings with time and experience.

First, let's draw the left side sword handle. As mentioned in the Iron Man tutorial, I always draw from top to bottom, and left to right to avoid holding my hand on the finished parts of the drawing. For this handle, you will need a black pencil to draw the shadowed part of the handle. Draw vertical gaps, and try to make them the same distance apart.

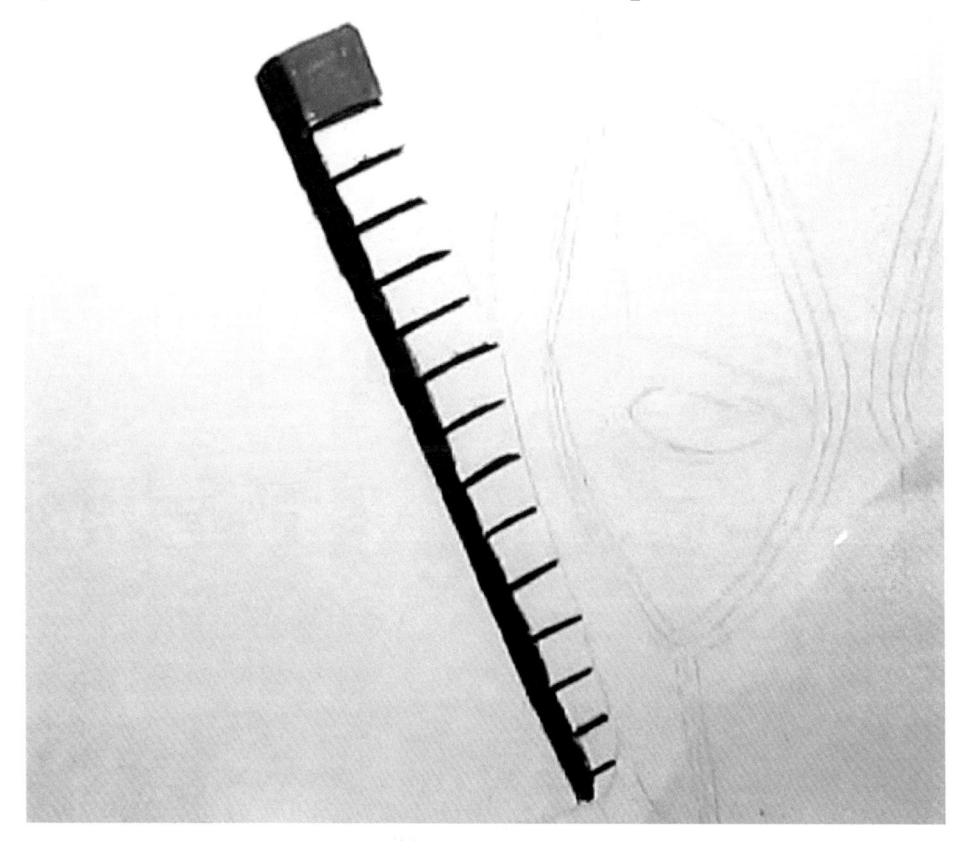

Now fill between the gaps with Warm Grey 50%. If you don't have this pencil, you can use any other mid-tone grey. Blend the edge between shadowed, black and grey parts with Warm Grey 70% and 90%.

Next, outline the left side eye using a well-sharpened Black and draw the corners of the white part of the mask in Cool Grey 10%.

How to draw realistic movie characters with colored pencils   Page 66

Draw the darkest parts of the leather around the eye in Black. Analyze the next image to see where to fill the black color.

If you're unsure, use a graphite pencil first, as Black cannot be fully erased. Press really hard to get an absolute black color. Color carefully around his eye to make sure the line between the black and white is clear and precise.

Then, color the highlight of the leather above his eye, in Cool Grey 30%.

Draw the area next to Cool Grey 30% in Cool Grey 50%, and as you reach the inner corner of his eye, use Cool Grey 70%. Blend the colors together to achieve a gradation.

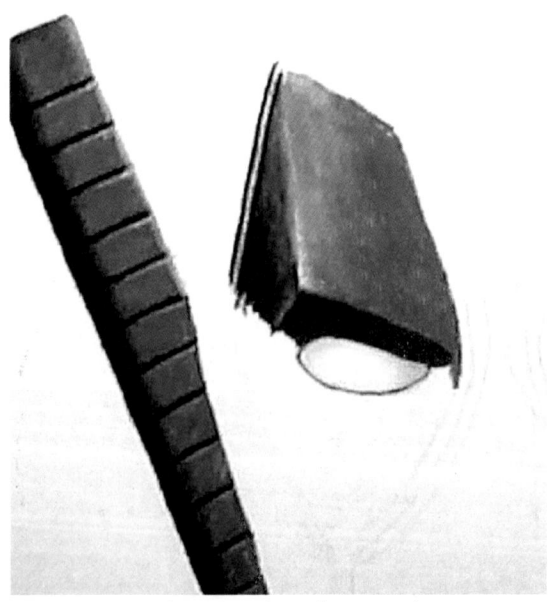

Using well-sharpened Black, draw the two sewing lines

How to draw realistic movie characters with colored pencils   Page 68

around the leather and inside the leather. Color between the lines with Cool Grey 30%.

Now draw the areas under his eye that get the most light in Cool Grey 30%.

How to draw realistic movie characters with colored pencils

Using Black, draw between the highlights and the eye, and blend with a well-sharpened Cool Grey 50%. The strongest shadows and highlights don't have a clear, sharp edge, but gradually flow into each other. Always blend the edges, particularly when drawing the leather.

Fill the left side of his eye, and draw the double line of stiches with Cool Grey 90%.

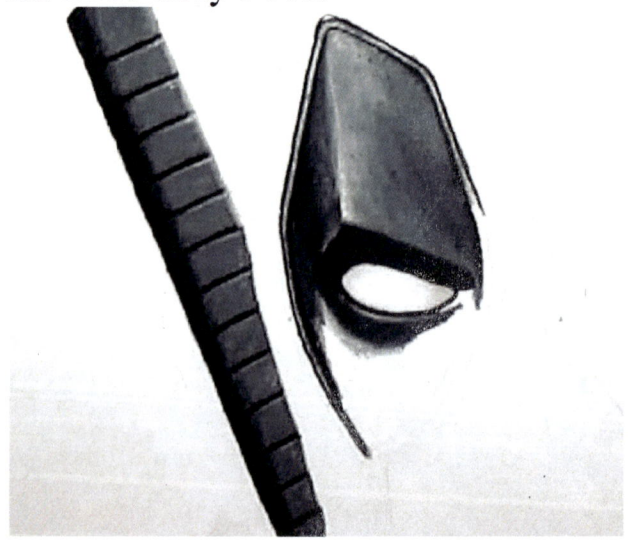

Next, draw the double row of stiches all around the leather with Black or Cool Grey 90% and fill in between with Cool Grey 20%.

Draw the right side of the area under his eye in Cool Grey 70%. This area gets more light and has to be slightly brighter than the right side.

How to draw realistic movie characters with colored pencils

Then fill the rest of area with Cool Grey 90%. Bright and dark colors don't have clear edges, so blend them with Cool Grey 50%.

As a mid-tone, this pencil won't brighten the edges of dark areas much, and won't darken the edges of bright areas much either. You can go over with black or white or another Grey to improve mistakes.

If you've followed the instructions, and your result doesn't look like mine but you can't figure out what's wrong, don't worry. You can make any improvement while you're drawing. If you are absolutely not satisfied and happy with your result so far, you may be best to start a new one from the very beginning. The more you try, the better you will understand your mistakes and what you need to improve or do differently.

Now move to the right eye. As with the left eye, start by shaping the white area of the eyeball and drawing in the corners with Cool Grey 20% and 10%. You could use a blending stump or tortillon for this. You can easily erase this if you want to change something. Outline it with a well-sharpened Black.

Draw the double stiches on the left upper side and shade in between with Cool Grey 30%.

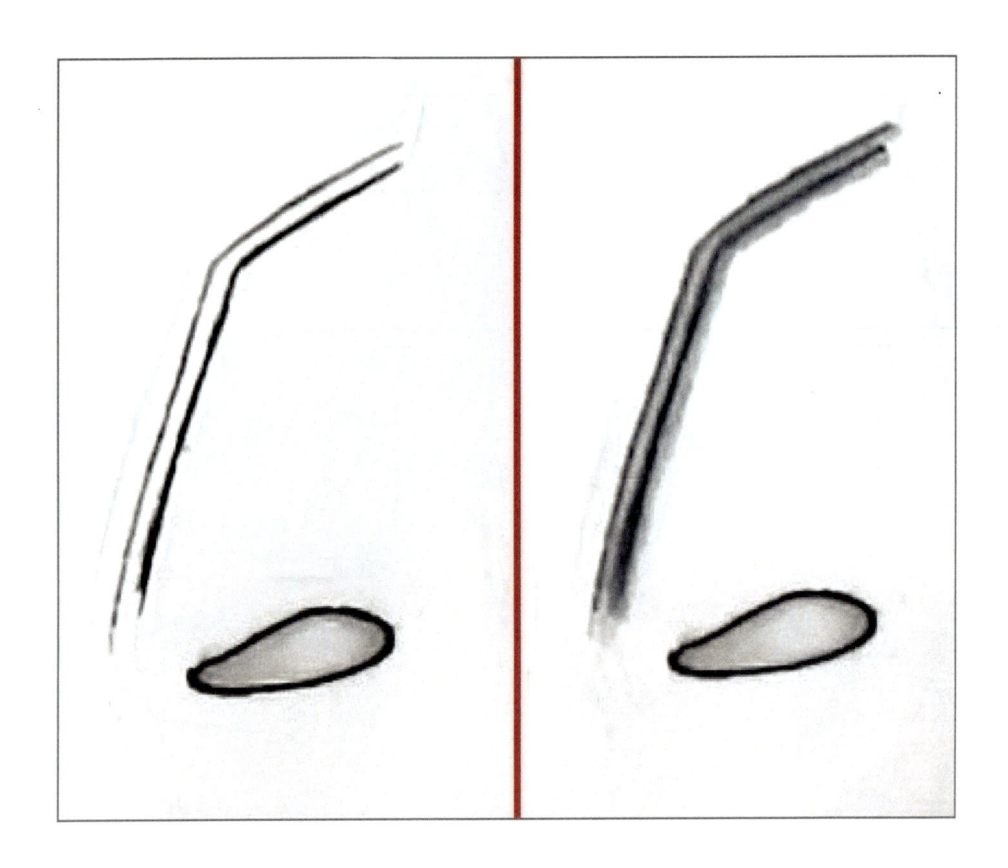

Fill the whole upper area with Black except for the leather that is bended on the right side. Press hard using Black since this has to be an absolute black.

Create the highlight above the eyes or "eyebrow" with Cool Grey 20% or 30% and create a tiny line over the black. If you cannot make a bright enough highlight, you may want to clear the top layer of color, since it already has picked up a lot of black, and create more highlight with clear top. Or you could use Cool Grey 10% or White if you cannot achieve it with a darker nuance of grey.

Use the same steps under the left eye. Draw two rows of stiches and fill with Cool Grey 70%, blending the tiny parts between the Black and Cool Grey 70% with a Cool Grey 90%.

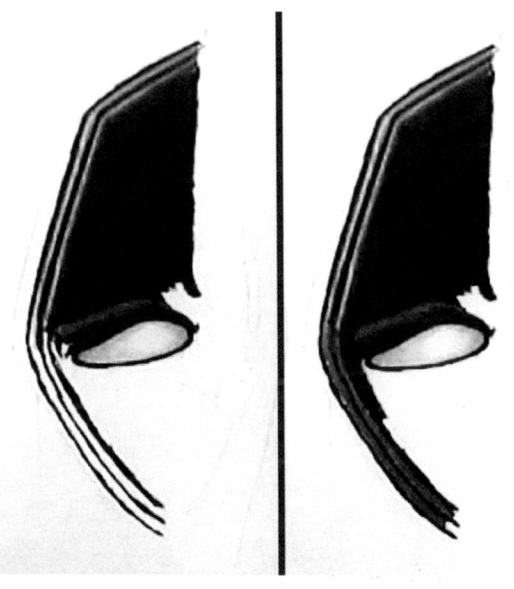

Fill the whole area under the eye with Black, except for the bended area of the leather that we left untouched when we drew the upper area. This area is highlighted and we won't use Black for it.

The area under the right eye is in absolute shadow so you don't have to create highlights here but can leave it like this.

Outline the vertical highlighted area of the leather on the right side with Black or Cool Grey 90%. As an always, if you're not confident, use a graphite pencil and go over it with Black when you are happy with your result.

Fill the whole area in Cool Grey 30%, and blend between this area and the surrounding Black, with Cool Grey 50% or 70%. If it's not bright enough, you can easily lighten this highlight with Cool Grey 10% or White over it.

Use the technique of layering and burnishing in order to fill the tooth of the paper. Layer these grey colors one over another and use circular motions to create a smooth texture. Watch the edges between the black and highlights and make them blurry. If necessary darken the highlights with Cool Grey 30%.

How to draw realistic movie characters with colored pencils

Next, you can start drawing the red part of the suit on his head. I couldn't find appropriate color for this, so I decided to mix Magenta with Crimson Red. It rarely happens that you can achieve the color you need with just one color; often you will have to create them. Prismacolor Premier makes only 150 colors which is a lot of pencils, but consider how many nuances exist that cannot be created with just one pencil.

You can't see them in the videos, but I always have pieces of paper around my drawings, and just like a painter, I use them to mix and test colors before I apply them. Since I use colors that are difficult to erase, I make sure that I'm using the right color. This is how I rarely make mistakes.

How to draw realistic movie characters with colored pencils

So, play with colors and nuances, mix them up and you'll work out how to create the color you need for your drawing. You can use my colors for these drawings, but you will have to figure them out for your own. It is very interesting, and you can learn a lot about colors this way.

For the first, basic layer use Magenta. You don't have to press hard or to burnish this color, as you will use one more color which will make the texture smoother. The fabric of the red parts of his suit is not as smooth as the leather, so you don't have to press hard or fill the tooth of the paper. Use Dark Umber or Black Raspberry to create stiches over the red fabric around the black leather.

Fill the whole of his forehead and create a double row of stiches above the top corners of his leather eye patches. Take a look at the next image to note where I've drawn them.

You don't have to change the pressure on your pencil while drawing this area with Magenta, since you are going to create shadows and highlights later on.

Now draw a second layer of color over the right side of his head, between its edge and the leather using Crimson Red. You can see how different the color is, and that the drawing is becoming three dimensional. This area can be smooth since the viewer cannot see the texture of the fabric from this perspective.

How to draw realistic movie characters with colored pencils

Next, create the shadows over his forehead in Black Raspberry and Dark Umber. Start over the area above the leather that is in the deepest shadow. The light is coming from the left, so the right side of his head should be darker, and the left brighter.

The upper area of the head is always brighter than the lower area, under his eyes and nose. Keep these facts in mind when creating the highlights and shadows.

Create another layer over the whole area in Crimson Red.

Using White, draw highlights on the left side of his forehead. Analyze my next image to see where the shadows and highlights are; you can see that his head looks round. Create the highlights and shadows along all the stiches.

If you see a white film build up on your drawing (that you can also notice in my pictures) don't worry. This happens when the wax from the pencil rises to the surface. Prismacolor also often forms a white haze called wax bloom a short time after the drawing is finished.

Simply wipe away with a cloth and spray with workable fixative.

If this doesn't bother you, use final fixative at the end of the drawing to prevent the wax build-up. At this point you cannot rework anything.

Workable fixative allows you to add more layers by coating the surface with a "tooth". I use a matte fixative for my colored pencil drawings. You can chose a workable fixative that you can still work on your drawing after spraying with it or you can use a final, non-workable fixative that you spray on your drawing when you are sure that you don't want to make any changes and before you frame it.

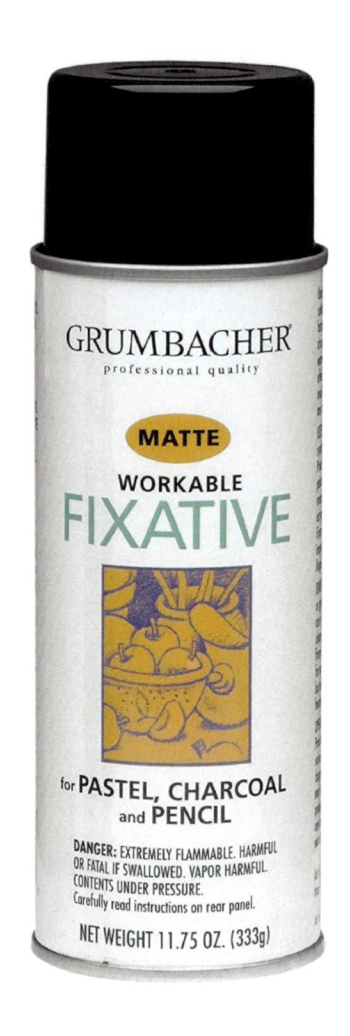

If you are satisfied with the upper part of the head you can move to the lower area. Start by mapping the stiches in Dark Brown or Black. As always, you can start with a graphite pencil. You will be still able to see it through the layer of the red color.

Using Magenta, draw the area under the left eye patch and the nose. Add another layer in Crimson Red. Create the shadow on the right side of his nose in Dark Umber or Black Raspberry. These are good color matches for darkening this red fabric.

Next, draw the right side of his head in Magenta and Crimson Red, and highlight the edge using White. It doesn't have to be a strong highlight, just a little bit to make it different to the rest of the fabric covering his ear and the right part of his jaw.

Draw the double, vertical rows of stiches from the lowest corner of the black leather around his right eye.

To create the shadows on the right side of his nose and eye patch, shade with Dark Umber, pressing lightly to create the dark basic red.

Then fill this area with layers of Magenta and Crimson Red. If it's not dark enough, go over it again with Dark Umber, or if it's too dark, lighten it with Crimson Red or Magenta. These colors will "pick up" the substance of the previously used dark pencils.

How to draw realistic movie characters with colored pencils

Create the highlight over the top of his nose with White.
You don't have to create a highlight under his nose.

This area under his nose has to be heavy shaded. Use Dark Umber and Black Raspberry for this. Create the shadow over the edge of his chin and over the whole area under the right leather. Hold your pencil almost parallel to the paper to create the texture of the textil. As mentioned, this red textil shouldn't be smooth. If you want to make it even detailed, you can draw cross stiches with well-sharpened pencils.

Use black colored pencil to draw the vertical gaps of the sword handle on the right side and try to make the equal distance between them.

How to draw realistic movie characters with colored pencils   Page 89

Fill the whole handle with Warm Grey 50%, and create highlights under every notch with a well-sharpened Warm Grey 10% (image below left). Draw the right-side shadow in Warm Grey 70%. and add a bit of Warm Grey 70% above every notch (image below right).

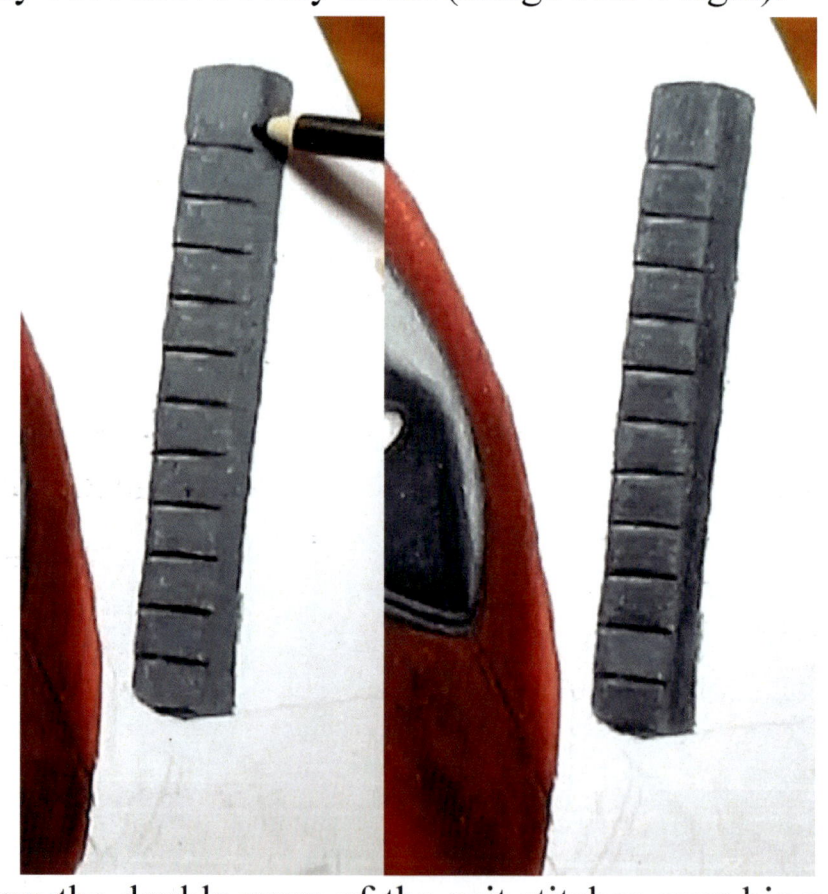

Draw the double rows of the suit stitches over his neck in Black or Dark Umber. Draw the shadowed area on the right side of his neck with Magenta, Crimson Red and Black Raspberry over the top. Use Black Raspberry and Black to underline his chin and make it pop up. Draw the leather belt under this red area in Warm Grey 90% for the shadowed parts and Warm Grey 70% for

How to draw realistic movie characters with colored pencils   Page 90

the rest. Use Warm Grey 10% to create highlights over the edges of the belt.

Now start to color the neck and the area between the neck and the leather of his shoulder in Magenta with a layer of Crimson Red over the top.

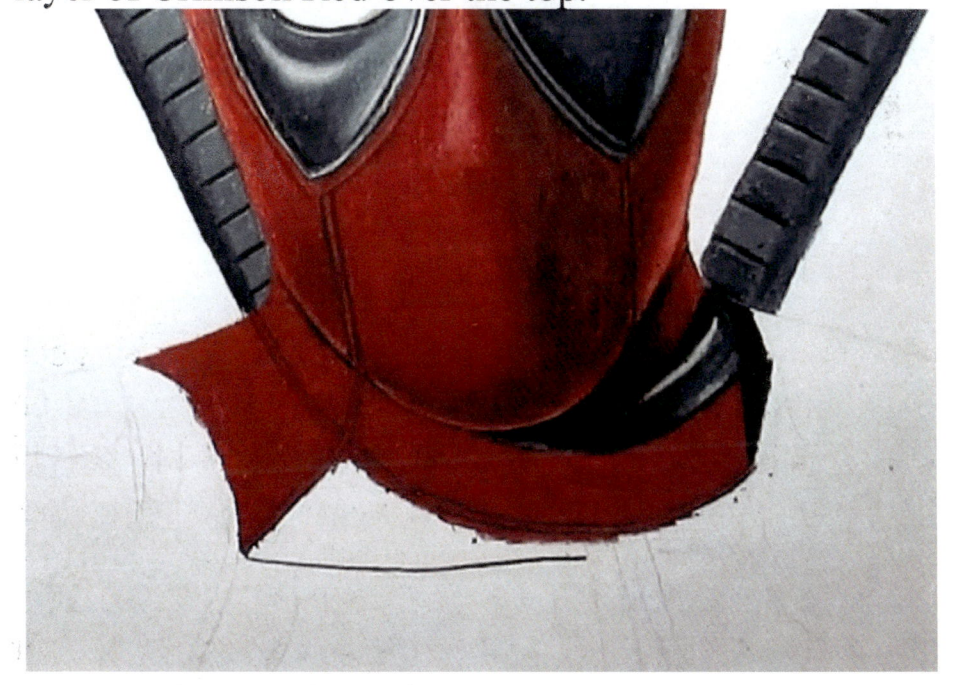

Create the shadowed parts on and under the left side of his chin with Dark Umber. Use a well-sharpened Dark Umber to strengthen the stiches, and White to create the highlight between the stiches.

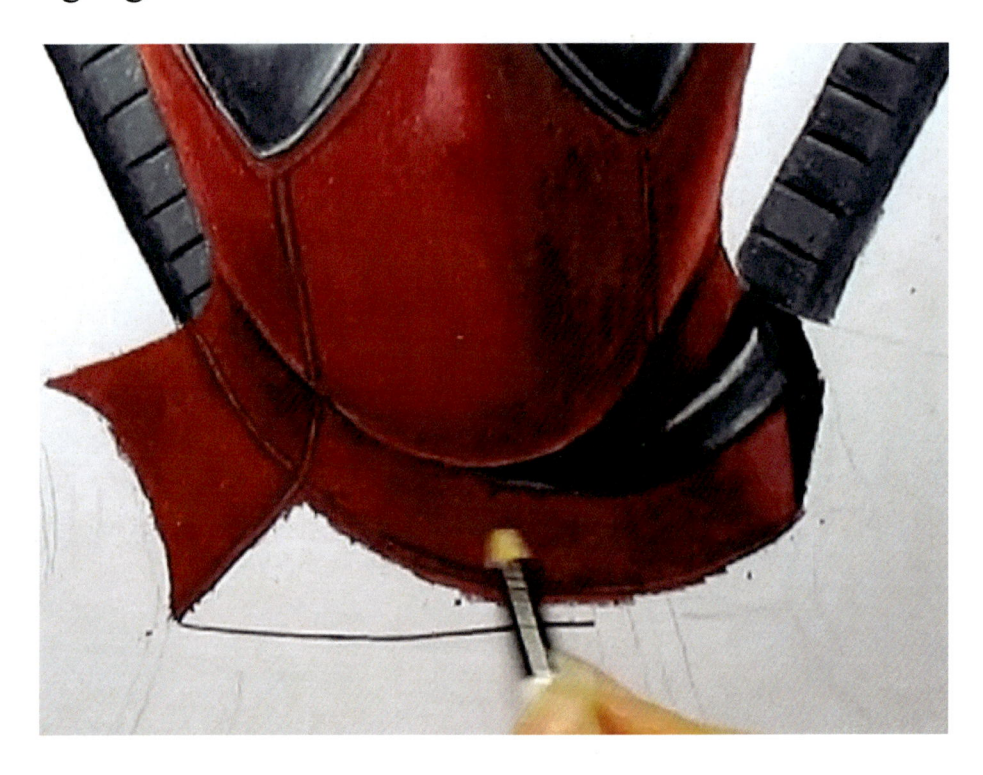

Next, create the stiches over the leather of his right shoulder and start to color it with Warm Greys. I suggest creating a flawless grey color gradation.

Start with the brightest part on the top of his shoulder that gets the most light using Warm Grey 10%, and as you color downwards, swap to Warm Grey 20%, then 30% and then 50%.

Next, strengthen the stiches with Black and draw the lower part of the leather around his shoulder in Warm Grey 90% and 70%. If you have used too much dark grey, you can lighten it with Warm Grey 50% or 30%. Draw tiny lines for highlights along the stiches in Warm Grey 30%.

Continue to draw the leather between the rounded part of the shoulder and the red fabric over his neck in Warm Grey 50%. Use a well-sharpened Black to create a gap between the two materials.

Using the same Warm Grey 50%, draw the rest of the leather under his shoulder.

Next, using Dark Brown or Black Raspberry, strengthen the stiches over the left part of his chest.

Fill the area of red fabric with Magenta. In the next image, you can see that the rows of stiches show through the layer of Magenta. You don't have to make it smooth since the texture of the red fabric isn't smooth.

How to draw realistic movie characters with colored pencils

Add a layer of Crimson Red. Create the highlights between the stiches with a well-sharpened White, and if necessary, darken the stiches with Dark Brown, or in the stronger shadow with Black.

Sometimes, as you draw new areas you will smudge previously drawn ones, or dust them with colored pencil particles, particularly the black and other dark areas. It is good practice to go over these areas one more at the end of the drawing process. This way you clean the dust and refresh the dark colors.

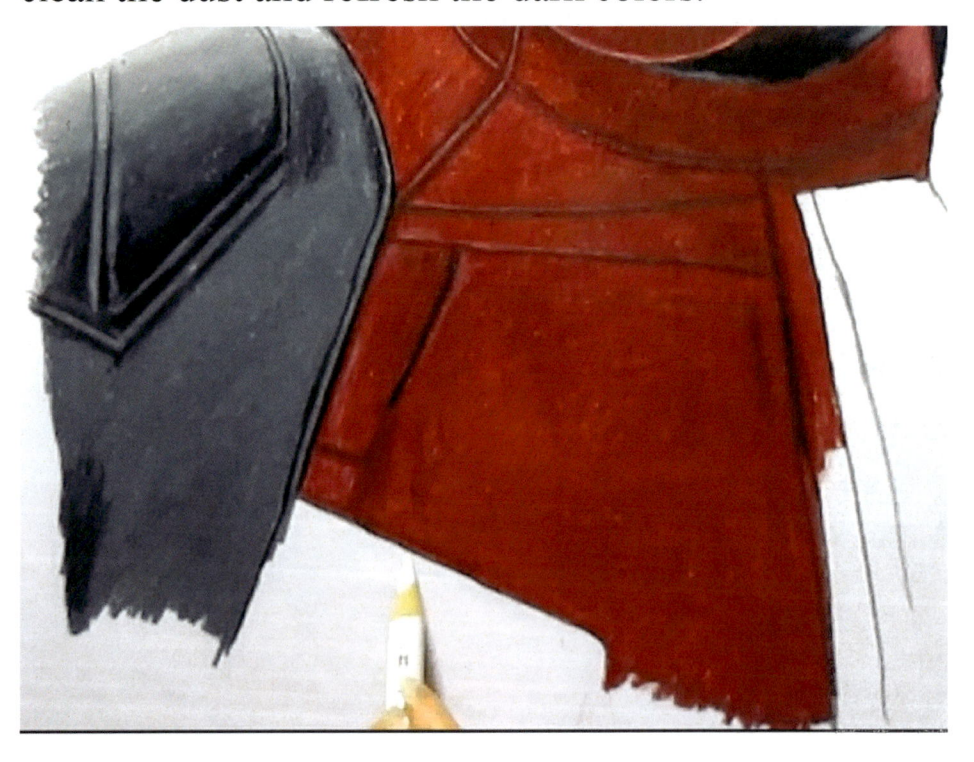

Do the same on the tiny visible area of the right side of his chest. Make first layer with Magenta.

Go over it with Crimson Red and create the shadows using Black raspberry.

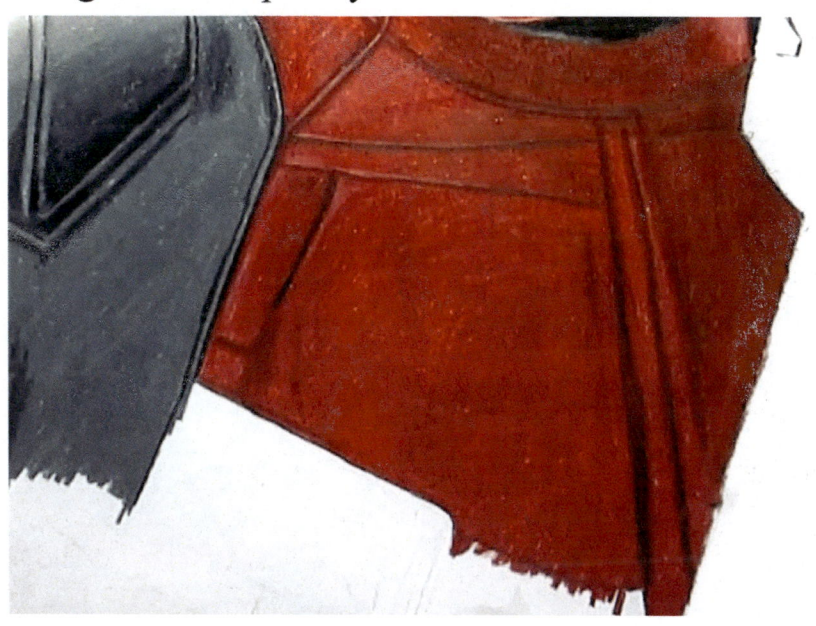

Create the vertical highlights in the middle of the chest in White.

Now draw the grey buckle on the left side of his chest, under the previously drawn red area, next to his arm. Strengthen the outlines in Black or Warm Grey 90%.

Use Warm Grey 30% as the basic color and fill the whole buckle coloring over the previously drawn black lines. They will be still visible under the layer of Warm Grey 30%. Try to make this area as smooth as possible.

Now add a darker layer over the whole area except for the highlights, with Warm Grey 50%. Examine the pictures carefully before you start applying the color. Use Warm Grey 20% for the highlights.

The creamy texture of Prismacolor Premier pencils makes it easy to create highlights over dark areas with gentle pressure. Always clean the tip with tissue or wiping on another piece of paper to remove the dark color from the bright pencil to ensure it can create new highlights easily. Experiment with different pressures on a separate piece of paper to see how this works for you. It is interesting to read drawing tips and tricks, but they are useless until they apply them to your drawing.

Next, strengthen the black lines again using Black, and smooth the whole buckle if necessary with your Warm Grey 30% basic color.

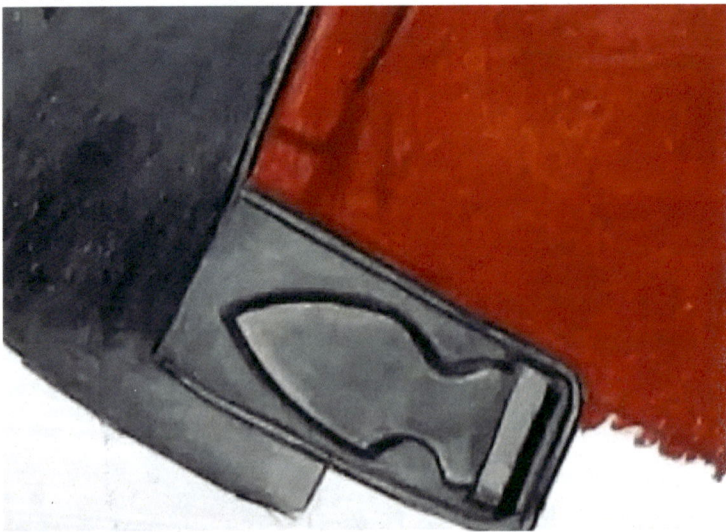

Next, draw the leather over his right shoulder with Warm Grey 30%. Fill the whole area.

Repeat the same on the right shoulder, and try to create gradation of the Warm Grey. Start with 10% and 20% on the top, and as you move downwards use the darker nuances of 30%, 50% and lastly 70%.

Now you can move onto the belt that starts under the leather of his shoulder. Look at one of your own belts to see how the texture looks. Draw this belt using basic color Warm Grey 30%, and the shadow under the leather of the shoulder in Black.

Draw short horizontal lines over the belt with Warm

Grey 90% to create the appropriate texture. Draw the strong shadow on the right side of the belt in Black.

Now fill the rest of the red fabric on the right side of his chest with Magenta.

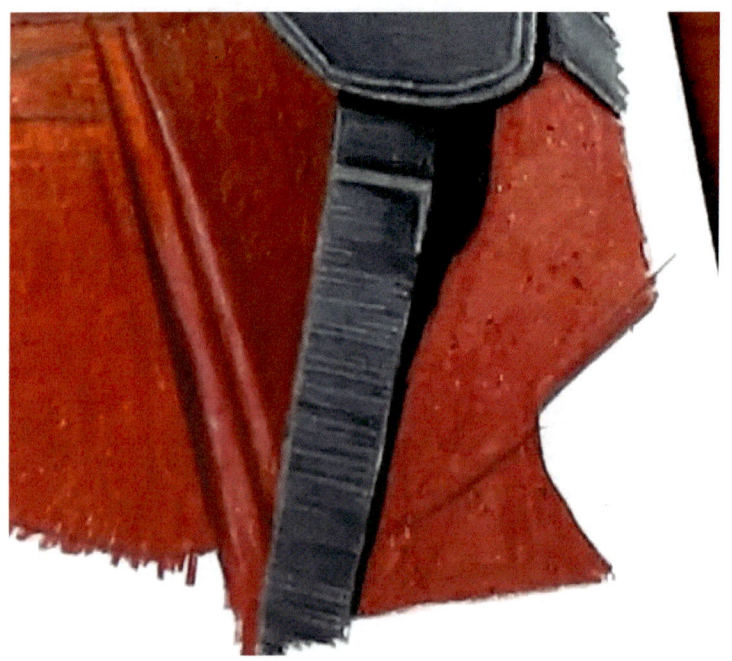

As always, add another layer of Crimson Red. This area gets less light, so create a stronger shadow with Black Raspberry, pressing harder on the right side of this area. Start creating the buckle on the right side by strengthening the outlines using Black.

Next, just as you did on the left, use Warm Grey 30% to fill the whole buckle. This texture has to be smooth, so draw in small circles.

If the grey texture of the buckle doesn't look smooth enough, **stipple** to fill the tiny gaps. Stippling is a technique of filling a space with small dots or specks. You can use it to equalize color shading, or to change the appearance of an object's solidity.

You may find a magnifier useful for this, as you can see more detail, place your dots more precisely, and stop before you possibly add too much shadow. This can take a lot of time, but try it to see if it fits your style.

Final, scanned drawing:

Watch drawing video on YouTube:
https://youtu.be/0gu8aMkkcO4

How to draw realistic movie characters with colored pencils

If you want to learn to draw Spider-Man, Superman and Batman, check out my book on Amazon:
"How to draw Superheroes"
https://www.amazon.com/dp/B00WUPNQVI/

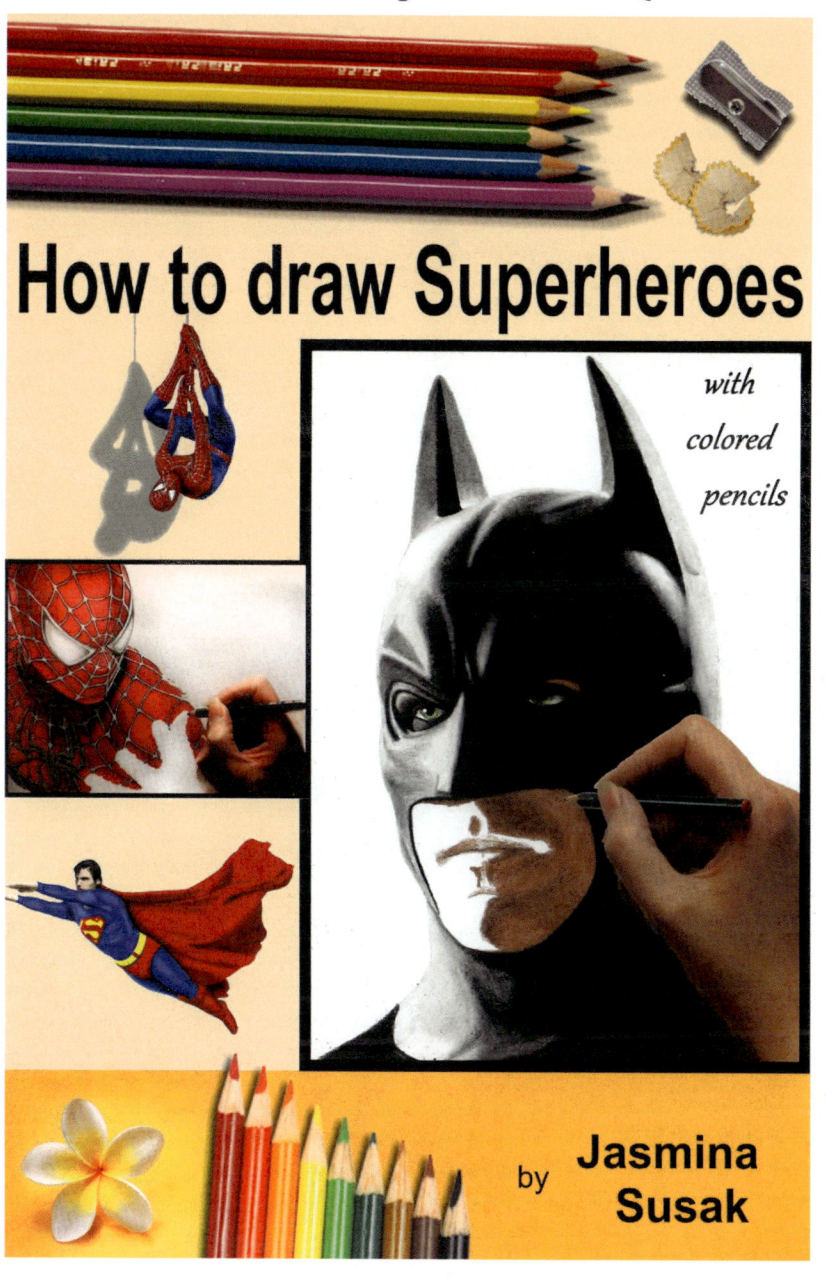

About Artist

Jasmina Susak is a self-taught, colored pencil artist and art teacher. Besides, she creates websites (including her own) as a hobby. She lives and works in Hungary. Visit her website for free tutorials, gallery, product links, drawing videos and more info:

jasminasusak.com

Facebook: https://www.facebook.com/JasminaSusakArt/

Instagram: https://www.instagram.com/jasminasusak/

Amazon Kindle: https://www.amazon.com/Jasmina-Susak/e/B00R9Y1ZW2/

DeviantART: http://jasminasusak.deviantart.com/

YouTube: https://www.youtube.com/user/JASMINA518/

Society6: https://society6.com/jasminasusakprints

Made in the USA
Middletown, DE
12 November 2017